POVERTY: ROWNTREE REVISITED

Poverty: Rowntree Revisited

SEAN STITT
DIANE GRANT
Liverpool John Moores' University

Avebury
Aldershot · Brookfield USA · Hong Kong · Singapore · Sydney

Published by
Avebury
Ashgate Publishing Limited
Gower House
Croft Road
Aldershot
Hants GU11 3HR
England

Ashgate Publishing Company
Old Post Road
Brookfield
Vermont 05036
USA

British Library Cataloguing in Publication Data

Stitt, Sean
Poverty: Rowntree Revisited
I. Title II. Grant, Diane
362.5

ISBN 1 85628 402 6

Printed and Bound in Great Britain by
Athenaeum Press Ltd, Newcastle upon Tyne.

Contents

List of tables

Acknowledgements

The authors would like to acknowledge the support and advice rendered by a number of individuals and groups. Within the Centre for Consumer Research in Liverpool John Moores' University, we greatly appreciate the time and effort taken by colleagues in gathering the data and arriving at the estimates contained in this book - particularly, Cath Fleet, Allan Hackett, Margaret Jepson, Anne Miller, Jennifer Miller, Elaine Prisk and ex-student Chris Owens, as well as secretarial support from Mary Harris and the encouragement from Jenny Peel and Jennifer Latto, Dave McEvoy and Ian Cook.

A variety of groups in the Merseyside community contributed valuable assistance, especially Kirkby Unemployment Centre, Merseyside Social Services Family Centres and Stewart Angus from the NSPCC.

Intellectual direction, constructive criticism and information material came from John Veit-Wilson of Newcastle upon Tyne University.

Of course, we express our gratitude to all the families who took part in the survey, but especially Roy and Christine Topping.

At various stages of the research, we presented our data and estimates to a number of conferences - Social Policy Assoc., Medical Sociology Group, the Public Sphere conference organised by the University of Salford, the British Sociological Assoc., the Annual Research Conference of Home Economics and Consumer Studies etc. We truly appreciate all the helpful comments and feedback at these conferences and took account of all the advice offered.

Special thanks is due to Kwik Save Group Plc for its very kind and generous support for the continuation of the proposed research.

Introduction

There are a number of facets to the concept of social citizenship and the levels of empowerment entailed. Relative notions of deprivation have exposed the exclusion of low income households from 'social life'. But clearly an even greater loss of citizenship rights and disempowerment is involved in a life of **primary poverty** - inadequate food, cold homes, ragged clothing etc. This research aims to **step into Seebohm Rowntree's shoes** and establish a primary poverty line for Britain in 1992 for a 'moderate family' of adult male, adult female and two young children. This poverty line will then be applied to official income data to determine the extent of such poverty and this will be compared to the findings of Rowntree in 1899, 1936/41 and 1950.

The central task of the research is to employ a **heuristic** measurement of poverty - i.e., 'primary poverty' - adopted originally for this purpose by Rowntree and to draw such a poverty line for 1992 which will be used to measure the extent of this type of deprivation in Britain. The task is not another phrasemongering attempt to propose a different, more complex, more esoteric model of measuring poverty. The object of the exercise is to accept, as Rowntree did, the arena for analysis set by the policy making process as the terms of reference for the debate. Rowntree founded his studies upon the same approach - his primary poverty line was constructed so that not even the most vehement critics of his conclusions could accuse him of including non-necessities in his weekly subsistence standards or of grinding a political axe.

Rowntree published the results of his major studies in 1901, 1936/41 and 1951. In each he drew a primary poverty line and measured the numbers of people living on or below this standard in the city of York. Each time, he found poverty was decreasing as the nation prospered. Pilot studies carried out by the authors recently (See Stitt 1992) suggest that this book will show a substantial nation-wide **increase** in primary poverty - i.e., an inability to afford necessities for physical efficiency in 1992. The aim is to allow those who would deny the existence of such deprivation to determine the measurement and then to test this against official data. A subsistence food minimum will be drawn up using the opinions and calculations of expert nutritionists. A primary fuel poverty line will be constructed by employing guidelines issued by the government's own statutory energy body. The clothing index will be the product of gathering opinions from 'poor' (Income Support) households as to their ideas of a minimum wardrobe stock and clothing costs. The sundries element will involve using Rowntree's judgements to draw up an informed, 'professional' estimate of the minimum personal and household sundry necessities required for a subsistence lifestyle in 1992.

Then these calculations will be aggregated into a weekly income level for an adult couple with two children aged eleven and under, not as a recommendation or prescription, but simply to argue that the extent of primary poverty in Britain today - i.e., that which is measured by an income level below which a poverty lifestyle is inescapable, regardless of frugality or providence - is comparable to the extent of such poverty as uncovered by Rowntree in 1899 and throughout the first half of the 20th century. The research does not explicitly urge a particular policy response, other than the obvious ones of radical increases in the income levels of the poor and a major re-evaluation of the poor relief scale rates and their relationship with an estimate of needs. Rather the research attempts to dismiss the official response to the poverty question - i.e., it is largely the result of households mismanaging an otherwise adequate income. The primary poverty line drawn here is so meagre and parsimonious that families on or below such an income simply cannot afford an adequate standard of living - their poverty is caused by structural forces not personal weaknesses, caused by inadequate government economic mismanagement, not by household financial mismanagement.

> Poverty is not only about shortage of money. It is about rights and relationships; about how people are treated and how they regard themselves; about powerlessness and the loss of dignity. Yet the lack of an adequate income is at its heart. 'Faith in the City', Church House 1985.

1 The poverty studies of B.S. Rowntree

In 'Poverty: A Study of Town Life' (1901), Rowntree established his aims quite succinctly and in a forthright manner: 'My object, in undertaking the investigation detailed in this volume was, if possible, to throw some light upon the conditions which govern the life of the wage-earning classes in provincial towns, and especially upon the problem of poverty.' (p.vii) Note that he did not refer to defining or measuring poverty or deprivation. He merely wished to 'throw some light' on the problem of poverty. His interest in publishing the causes of poverty stretched as far only as inadequacy of income or unwise expenditure. He asked: 'How much of it, (poverty), was due to insufficiency of income and how much to improvidence? How many families were sunk in a poverty so acute that their members suffered from a chronic insufficiency of food and clothing?' (p.viii)

Above Rowntree referred to 'a poverty' (as opposed to 'poverty') so deep that the poor could not afford the basic necessities of life. He was not defining nor measuring 'poverty' - rather he was dealing with **a type of poverty**, so described. He went on to explain his methodological approaches. A central aim of his investigation was to determine firstly, the proportion of the population living in a certain type of poverty; and secondly, the nature of that poverty. He divided the population so living into two classes:

(a) families whose total earnings were insufficient to obtain the minimum necessaries for the maintenance of merely physical efficiency. Poverty falling under this heading, he described as 'primary' poverty;

(b) families whose total earnings would have been insufficient for the maintenance of merely physical efficiency were it not that some portion of it was absorbed by other expenditure, either useful or wasteful. Poverty falling under this heading was described as 'secondary' poverty. (p.ix/x)

To measure the proportion living in primary poverty, he needed to know the weekly income of each family and 'the minimum sum necessary to maintain families of various sizes in a state of physical efficiency'. To do this, he carried out preliminary research into the amounts and types of food which, with reference to the most recent and comprehensive tests, were deemed necessary within those terms of reference. He also needed to acquire data on the actual rents paid and a complex estimate of the required spending upon all items other than nutrition and housing. (p.x)

In Chapter VIII, Rowntree examined 'workmen's budgets and especially the diets of the working classes'. He recognised that nutritional quality was 'so intimately associated with the problem of poverty' that he felt compelled to investigate it in much more detail than other areas of subsistence need. He sought precise information on the quantity, character and cost of the food consumed by, initially, 18 families belonging to his various layers of the working class, from the poorest to the better-off. His information spanned periods from one week to two years, with the majority of the budgets being kept for at least three weeks, with the greatest care was taken to ensure accuracy.

He divided the population of York into seven groupings, according to income levels, with group A being the poorest. He explained that the poverty of class (A) (under 18 shillings a week for a 'moderate family') was rendered apparent when it was acknowledged that it would have cost £227.15s.8d. to provide **food** alone for these people for one week, according to the diet allowed to paupers in York workhouse, calculating the cost at contract prices. The total earnings of the 474 families was thus shown to fall short by £21.17s.6d. of the sum required to provide **food alone** without taking into consideration other necessary expenditure such as that on clothes and fuel. (p.40) This led Rowntree to observe that: ' ... the food of these poor people is totally inadequate ... a glance at these will show how monotonous it is, consisting largely of a succession of bread, dripping and tea: bacon, bread and coffee, with only a little butcher's meat and none of the extras and bit little of the variety which serves to make meals interesting and appetizing.' (p.44) He concluded that it was evident that whatever objection may have been taken to the standard of food requirements he adopted, it could not be said that the standard was too high.

In introducing his subsistence 'primary poverty' cut-off point, he explained that he had to ascertain what income was required by families of different sizes to provide the minimum of food, clothing and shelter needful for the maintenance of merely physical health. But, he warned that, in pursuance of pre-empting criticisms of opponents of his poverty message: 'Expenditure for the development of the mental, moral and social sides of human nature will not be taken into account at this stage of the inquiry. Nor in thus estimating the poverty line will any account be taken of expenditure for sick clubs or insurance.' (p.87)

In addressing the extent of 'secondary poverty' in York, he went on to explain that to establish this by direct inquiry would have involved knowing in every case, the average sum spent weekly on 'drink, gambling or other wasteful expenditure and to ascertain also whether the wife was a thrifty housekeeper or the reverse'. (p. 115) As this was impractical to operationalise, Rowntree used observations and subjective judgements. Direct information was obtained from neighbours or from a member of the household concerned, 'to the effect that the father or the mother was a heavy drinker; in other cases, the pinched faces of the ragged children told their own tale of poverty and privation. Judging in this way, partly by appearance and partly from information given, I have been able to arrive at a fair estimate of the total number of persons living in poverty in York.' (p.115/6)

Rowntree then listed what he perceived to be the immediate causes of 'secondary poverty': drink, betting and gambling; ignorant or careless house-keeping and; other improvident expenditure, the latter often induced by irregularity of income. But, he concluded unambiguously, 'There can be little doubt that the predominant factor is drink.' (pp. 141/2) However, Rowntree was mindful that these 'immediate causes' of 'secondary poverty' were themselves sometimes the inevitable consequences of life in the slums, in abject poverty, in sometimes desperation and often hopelessness: 'Though we speak of the above causes as those mainly accounting for most of the "secondary poverty", it must not be forgotten that they themselves are often the outcome of the adverse conditions under which too many of the working classes live. Housed for the most part in sordid streets, frequently under overcrowded and unhealthy conditions, compelled very often to earn their bread by monotonous and laborious work, unable, partly through limited education and partly through overtime and other causes of physical exhaustion, to enjoy intellectual recreation, what wonder that many of these people fall a ready prey to the publican and the bookmaker? The limited horizon of the mother has a serious effect upon her children: their home interests are narrow and unattractive and too often they grow up to seek relief from the monotony of their work and their environment in the public house or in the excitement of betting.' (pp. 144/5)

In probably one of his most direct and (constructively) harsh presentations of exactly what his 'primary poverty' lifestyle involved, lest anyone should fail to grasp the reality of his message, he stated quite clearly: 'And let us clearly understand what a merely physical efficiency means. A family living upon the scale allowed for in this estimate must never spend a penny on railway fare or omnibus. They must never go into the country unless they walk. They must never purchase a halfpenny newspaper or spend a penny to buy a ticket for a popular concert. They must write no letters to absent children, for they cannot afford to pay the postage. They must never contribute anything to their church or chapel, or give any help to a neighbour which costs them money. They cannot save nor can they join a sick club or Trade Union, because they cannot pay the necessary subscription. The children must have no pocket money for dolls, marbles or sweets. The father must smoke no tobacco nor drink no beer. The mother must never buy any pretty clothes for herself or for her children, the character of the family wardrobe, as for the family diet, being governed by the regulation; "Nothing must be bought but that which is absolutely necessary for the maintenance of physical health and what is bought must be of the plainest and most economical description." Should a child fall ill, it must be attended by the parish doctor; should it die, it must be buried by the parish. Finally, the wage-earner must never be absent from his work for a single day. If any of these conditions are broken, the extra expenditure is met, and **can only be met**, by limiting the diet, or, in other words, by sacrificing physical efficiency.' (pp. 133/4)

In the 'Human Needs of Labour' (1936), Rowntree made an attempt to formulate a measuring rod to enable him to assess the wage necessary for physical efficiency. Although physical efficiency was still the core criteria for defining subsistence, he conceded that he had to cover the whole ground afresh, for socio-economic conditions had changed greatly during the intervening years since his 1899 study. The average size of the family was different and this affected his figures substantially. He accepted that much progress had been achieved on dietetics by physiologists and biochemists. Scientific knowledge on vitamins and the importance of a healthy dietary, a sufficiency of certain mineral salts, had been gathered and the dietary which was previously considered satisfactory was no longer so considered.

Stressing his commitment to as much scientific objectivity as was possible, he sought to conduct his 1936 inquiry on strictly scientific lines, without allowing his personal feelings to affect his judgement and, in doing so, he was convinced that his main conclusions could not be reasonably challenged. He concluded that, in assessing the cost of the various items necessary for the maintenance of merely physical efficiency, he calculated that these could not be provided at less than 53 shillings a week for an urban worker with a wife and three dependent children. This sum allowed scarcely for any margin, certainly not more than 3s./6d. a week ('little more than the cost of a cocktail') for holidays, beer and tobacco, amusements such as visits to a cinema or football match, travelling other than fares to and from work, or contingencies of any kind.

In a rare reference to his own implicit political beliefs and values, he made clear that the minimum income levels that he was attempting to address were founded upon basic physical requirements: 'In discussing the principles on which minimum wages should be fixed, we should draw a clear distinction between **minimum** wages and wages above the minimum. The former should be determined primarily by human needs, the latter by the market value of the services rendered.' The first step he took in fixing minimum wages was therefore to establish 'the human needs of the workers'. He could then proceed to discuss the costs of providing for these needs. (p. 15)

He then continued his inquiry into another publication five years later, 'Poverty and Progress' (1941). The title implies that he was concerning himself with measuring the impact of economic prosperity and social advancement on levels of poverty and deprivation. He explained this in his usual rationale: 'In every well-conducted business, a balance sheet based on a physical stock-taking is prepared periodically: if this were not done, it would be impossible accurately to assess the measure of success which had been attained. This book is intended to help those interested in social well-being to measure the degree in which a typical provincial city has benefited from the efforts put forth during this century to improve social conditions.' (p. v) The question he sought to answer was what proportion of the population was living in poverty. In order to do this, it was necessary to fix a poverty line and for the purpose of his latest inquiry, he adopted as his poverty line, the standard of living attainable by a family of man, woman and three dependent children having an income of 43s./6d. a week (at 1936 prices) after paying rent. This is the figure at which he arrived after careful investigation undertaken in connection with his book, 'The Human Needs of Labour'. And, with reference to the overall trends exposed by this investigation, he commented that in common with other social surveys which had been made at the same time, his 1941 study showed that conditions were immensely better than they were 30 or 40 years previous. 'But they are still far from being such as to justify any spirit of complacency on the part of those who care for the welfare of the people.' (p. ix)

Introducing his methodology, he clarified that his aim was to investigate every family in the city whose chief wage-earner was earning not more than £250 a year and the inquiry covered all the streets where such people were likely to be living. Again, in rationalising his endeavours to construct an almost indefensible minimum standard of living in order to prevent attacks from predictable quarters for including items which were not totally necessary, he adopted the lowest standard which responsible experts could justify. This held good of the other than food items entering into his cost of living, each of which was fixed only after making thorough inquiry into the minimum expenditure necessary. In this connection, he quoted what he had wrote in his 1936 book: 'Let me repeat that the standards adopted throughout this book err on the side of stringency rather than extravagance. I am convinced that the closest investigation would fail appreciably to lower any of my estimated costs. Indeed as I have pursued my investigation, I have been increasingly impressed by the fact that to keep a family of five in health on 53 shillings a week, even when income is guaranteed for 52 weeks a year, needs constant watchfulness and a high degree of skill on the part of the housewife. Moreover, practically the whole income is absorbed in providing the absolute necessaries of physical health. After these, and certain other indispensable items are provided for, there remains scarcely anything - certainly not more than 3s./4d. a week for "all else". Out of this must come all recreation, all luxuries, such as beer and tobacco, all travelling except that of the breadwinner to and from work, all savings for holidays - indeed almost every item of expenditure not absolutely required to maintain the family in physical health and there is no allowance for contingencies.' (p. 29)

Rowntree was mindful that insufficiency of income was not the sole difficulty nor the only criteria in generating poverty and thus, an increase in income, no matter how substantial, was not the only solution to the problem of poverty. Home economics and consumer knowledge was almost as important: 'It is true that, at 1936 prices, a family of five could be adequately fed for this sum (20s./6d.), but (and it is an important qualification), in order to achieve this end, the housewife must possess an unusual amount of knowledge of the nutritive value of various foodstuffs. Among the 28 families (studied in detail), not one succeeded in selecting a dietary anything like as economical as that used in our minimum standard of living. The inquiry ... points clearly to the fact that, to ensure a well-fed population, it is not enough to give every family the wherewithal to buy the foodstuffs necessary for health; they must also be shown what to buy. In a word, it points to the importance of widespread education in the science of dietetics.' (p. 173)

No attempt was made by Rowntree to measure 'secondary poverty' this time. He rationalised this by pointing to ever-changing social attitudes and a general liberalisation of understanding of problems like poverty. In this survey, he made no attempt to measure 'secondary poverty' by direct observation, partly because the method of doing this adopted by 1899 appeared to him in 1941 as being too rough to give reliable results and also because, even had he done so, the results would not have rendered possible, a comparison with 1899, for ideas of what constitutes 'obvious want and squalor' had changed profoundly since then. 'There is no doubt that, in 1899, investigators would not have regarded as "obvious want and squalor" conditions which would have been so regarded in 1936 and, on the other hand, a large proportion of the families living below the 1936 poverty line would not, in 1899, have been regarded as showing signs of poverty.' (pp. 460/1)

In his final major study, 'Poverty and the Welfare State', which he co-wrote with Laver (1951), he explained that the purpose of this book was to throw light on the question of how the various welfare measures which had come into force since 1936 had succeeded, if at all, in reducing poverty. 'If we made a social survey of York in 1950 on the same lines as those adopted in 1936, but dealing only with economic questions, we should have an accurate yardstick for measuring the comparative amount of poverty in York in those years.' (p. 1)

The most notable, and by far the most accurate social science commentator on the works of Rowntree has been Professor John Veit Wilson, who explained that Rowntree's standards were 'prescriptive', **not** in terms of prescribing 'how poor people in society ought to be able to live' (e.g. Beveridge 1942), but in the 'purported demonstration that poor people need more money than they are getting'. (e.g. Piachaud, Bradshaw, Stitt) (1987, p. 188) However, Veit Wilson went on to argue that primary poverty continued as an 'explicitly expert construction', even given Rowntree's caveat that 'it was not intended to be a prescription for a minimum income on which anyone could actually live a social life.' (1987, p. 188) Similarly, this research constitutes a heuristic exercise using a heuristic research instrument - the primary poverty line for 1992. Elsewhere, Veit Wilson (1986) provides a powerful and scathing attack on the widely misleading misrepresentations of Rowntree's approaches and conclusions, particularly that traditional interpretation of Rowntree's models as constituting the epitome of 'absolute poverty', as opposed to the 'relative deprivation' models of Townsend in 'Poverty in the UK' (1979). Veit Wilson introduces his arguments thus: 'Townsend's achievement was a paradigmatic shift, not from absolutist to relativistic models of poverty, but from relativistic models based on standards perceived by expert observers (Rowntree) to relativistic models based on standards derived from the whole population by social surveys (Townsend).' (1986, p. 69)

For those who had mistakenly believed that Rowntree had prescribed a poverty line income, a weekly sum of money that would constitute an acceptable and/or adequate lifestyle if spent wisely, Veit Wilson had this to say: 'His development of the primary poverty measure in 1899 was explicitly a heuristic device and not a policy prescription ... It is a common error among authors to assume that, in 1899, Rowntree used an income measure to identify and measure the poor. Such authors suggest that they are unclear about Rowntree's important distinction between the identifying criteria of poverty and the heuristic device of a primary poverty measure.' (1986, pp. 70/72) Similarly, there is no policy prescription involved in the estimates of this book; but, of course, as with Rowntree's works, there are clear policy implications. Veit Wilson alleges that some authors perceived that Rowntree's 'poor' in their entirety were living below the primary poverty level, when, in fact, only one-third of them were, the remainder of 'the poor' living on incomes above Rowntree's primary poverty standard. Thus, for Rowntree, 'the poor' were much more than those in primary poverty and an adequate 'poverty line income' was much more than his primary poverty standard. Presented diagrammatically:

(1) the 'poor' - identified by criteria of poverty, less than half of the working class were poor;
(2) those living below Rowntree's primary poverty line - one-third of the 'poor' had incomes below Rowntree's primary poverty line;
(1) minus (2) = secondary poverty (Rowntree 1901, p. 117).

The 'poor' identified by criteria of poverty were those 'living in obvious want and squalor'. All of these households were visited. Rowntree then subtracted those living on or below his primary poverty line from the numbers of people 'living in obvious want and squalor' to arrive at those living in 'secondary poverty'. Put succinctly: 'The distinction between primary and secondary poverty was not designed to identify the poor but was intended to "illuminate the nature of that poverty" - "that poverty" being conceptually distinct from either primary or secondary poverty and consisting of the characteristics of families identified by the investigators as being poor. It is essential to note that the precise criteria used by Rowntree's investigators to determine which members of York's working class were and were not poor **did not include income** ... (they) were not financial; they were behavioural and visible. In the body of the 1901 volume, Rowntree elaborated (this) method to give greater depth to the meaning of "obvious want and squalor".' Rowntree stated clearly that these identifications of who was poor did not thereby define any particular income level as the poverty line. A family might have maintained the outward appearance of not being poor, whilst having an income less than that of families which did not maintain this appearance. Diagrammatically:

Rowntree's Concepts of Poverty 1899:
The Whole Population consisting of
The Non-Poor
distinguished by lifestyle from
The Poor (#P)
who consist of those people
In Secondary Poverty (P2)
who are distinguished **by income level** from those people In Primary Poverty (PI)
Procedurally speaking: #P - P1 = P2 ... YES
P1 + P2 = #P ... NO

This clear conscious distinction between poverty (which is a relative condition defined by visible lifestyle) and the primary poverty income level runs through Rowntree's works from the very outset. It is vitally important to clearly understand how Rowntree recognised the relativistic nature of the primary poverty line and his belief that such a standard was not in a general sense 'scientifically absolute': 'It is thus seen that the point at which "primary poverty" passes into "secondary poverty" is largely a matter of opinion, depending on the standard of well-being which is considered necessary.' (Rowntree 1901, p. 141)

Although Rowntree has been historically misread, misinterpreted and misrepresented, one researcher who grasped the fundamental nature of his studies was Bowley who was one of the most prolific of Rowntree's statistical contemporaries. Bowley exercised a number of studies in English towns using a form of the primary poverty line as the measuring instrument. But Bowley apparently did not labour under the misconceptions about the status of that instrument, any more than Rowntree did. Bowley wrote: 'Though this calculation appears to have a scientific basis, and as far as knowledge of nutrition goes is accurate, it is in fact conventional, rather than accurate.' (Bowley & Hogg 1925, p. 13) In tandem, the figures presented in this research exercise are conventional (1992) and are accurate only in terms of adhering to nutritional guidelines and the opinions of experts. Bowley seemed quite aware that the primary poverty line was not an income on which anyone could live: 'We are far from arguing that larger incomes are not to be desired ... We are only concerned here to establish a standard below which a family is prima facie in want.' (Bowley & Hogg 1925, p. 14) - prima facie meaning that there was no requirement at that low income level to debate other causes of poverty. Thus all the families in this study found to be in receipt of incomes which are below the primary poverty line are 'in want' - i.e., their poverty is caused immediately by inadequate incomes.

In addressing the question as to why Rowntree adopted this model/approach, Veit Wilson (1986) makes the following statement which encapsulates his comprehensive analysis and arguments about the nature of Rowntree's research approach in employing a rhetorical device for use as a political strategy:

> The problem of poverty at the end of the 19th century was not how to define it ... but to find out what the scale and causes were ... A conventional explanation of poverty, held by many among the middle classes, and exemplified by the work of the Charity Organisation Society, was that people who looked and acted poor did so because they wasted their money, not because they had too little of it. To test this assumption, one does not have to believe in the validity of a minimum subsistence approach oneself: it is enough if the proponents of the individualistic assumption are prepared to believe in it, as they generally were, as it had the stamp of approval of nutritional science on it. As a research chemist by training and practice, Rowntree wanted to use these respected and persuasive methods and language to find out which explanation was the most plausible. To do this, he had to see if there was any level of income at which the individualistic hypothesis could no longer hold true: that is, could there be an income level at which people could not maintain a non-poor lifestyle, no matter how hard they tried? Assuming for the sake of the experiment alone that all forms of social expenditure are disputable, but that scientifically-proven minimum subsistence expenditures are irreducible. Rowntree was able to show that one-third of the poor had incomes too low even to keep physically fit, and his contemporary critics agreed that poverty might be caused by individual improvidence: the question at issue was whether some of it was caused by too little income. (pp. 81/82)

This was the very essence and the heart of Rowntree's research and it must be understood that the question at the kernel of this 'scientific' research is: How much poverty in Britain in 1992 is caused by inadequate income? The answer to this will be provided, as Rowntree's answer was, by drawing a subsistence primary poverty line and measuring the numbers living on incomes below this standard. As has been stated, this project defines its terms of reference as estimating the extent of poverty, not defining the phenomenon. There is an official view of poverty which identifies its causes within individual irrational expenditure of an otherwise adequate income. By confining this exercise to examining the validity of these hypothesis does not indicate any academic justification or support for this model. Indeed, among the entire research team, there was not a single disciple of the minimum subsistence approach to measuring poverty. The fact of the matter is that the policy making process adhere to such an approach. The question of individual improvidence is not explicitly commented upon here: the crucial question addresses the extent of poverty caused **immediately** by insufficient incomes.

Thus the widespread criticisms of Rowntree have been that:
- he prescribed the primary poverty line income level as adequate to live on and;
- as a consequence, that, in considering only physical efficiency, he failed to take account of all social and psychological requirements.

Both of these attacks can be exposed as groundless and false when what Rowntree actually wrote is examined. Others, such as Frank Field (1982), have also recognised the kernel of Rowntree's strategy. He acknowledged that Rowntree perceived the need to counter any charge that his findings might exaggerate and thus his constant emphasis on a minimum subsistence approach. (p. 116) To illustrate this point, Rowntree stated that he purposely selected such a dietary so that no one could possibly accuse him of placing his subsistence level too high. This expression demonstrates how Rowntree selected his approach to convince those who required to be persuaded, not because he actually perceived that individuals could afford a social life on the primary poverty line, but because the policy-makers believed that such was possible. 'To accept an opponents premise for the sake of argument as the basis for one's criticism is a normal debating practice, but it has been turned against Rowntree.' (Veit Wilson 1986, p. 82)

Rowntree reinforces this message by explaining in 1951 that he assumed a poverty line so low as to be open to the criticism of serious inadequacy: 'I choose these criterion about merely physical efficiency because I did not want people to say that Rowntree's "crying for the moon"'. But there is no rational reason why anyone should have done so. The core observation was that Rowntree was employing his approaches to persuade even opponents of social reform of his conclusions. As he pragmatically wrote in 1941 of his 'Human Needs of Labour' poverty standard used in 1936: 'I purposely adopted a standard which the most hard-boiled critic could not say was extravagant. Had I given any justification for such a criticism, those who wanted to excuse the present state of things would have fastened on any items which might be regarded as extravagant and thus sought to neutralise the effect of my book.' (quoted in Briggs 1961, p. 296) Briggs clarifies the functionalism inherent in

Rowntree's approaches: 'As in 1901, however, the austerity of Rowntree's standards was more telling, at least to the better-off people, than a more generous analysis, tinged with what, in the 1930's, might still have been dismissed as "sentimentality"'. (Briggs 1961, p. 297) Tabulated by Veit Wilson:

'Essential' = 'merely physical efficiency' = 'immediate non-postponable physiological human needs' as opposed to 'postponable psychological human needs'. Rowntree was aware that both sets of needs could not be met simultaneously from an inadequate income. (Veit Wilson 1987, p. 85)

In posing the question as to why poor people spend their inadequate incomes on social recreational activities instead of food, Rowntree argued that working people are 'just as human' as those with more money. They could not live just on a 'fodder basis'. They also desired relaxation and recreation just as the rest of society does. But, he added, they could only afford these things by going short of something which was essential to physical fitness and so 'they go short and the national standard of health is correspondingly lowered.' (Rowntree 1936, pp. 126/7) That is, a healthy lifestyle could be achieved on such a low income, but only by crificing the satisfaction of conventional social and psychological needs. Thus Rowntree's central task was to show that poverty still existed even by the **doubters' yardsticks**. Similarly, the core objective of this research is to suggest the extent of primary poverty by employing the 'rule of thumb' assumed by those who wish to excuse the present state of income deprivation.

In 'Founders of the Welfare State' (1984), John Veit Wilson expressed his regret about Rowntree's misconceived contribution to the poverty debate: 'Since his death in 1984, B.S. Rowntree has been remembered better for ideas about poverty which he did not hold than for the better understanding of it which he pioneered'. (p. 75) Rowntree, the political being, was a Liberal who held that the state's power should be employed to establish minimum standards of living and to protect citizens from falling beneath them, to free them from the 'chance evils of the market'. (p. 75) And the practical and beneficial consequences of his works meant that politicians could no longer avoid responsibility for state policy action against what was perceived, by the end of the 19th century, as a substantial socio-economic problem - 'a threat to the nation's economic efficiency and political stability'. (p. 75) It is hoped that this research, when completed, will inform the policy making system of the failings of the free market as the appropriate arena for poverty prevention, will demonstrate the extent of structurally-induced poverty and will argue for policies aimed at radically increasing the incomes of the lower socio-economic groups. If a primary poverty rate of 9.91% of the entire population (as

Rowntree found in 1899) was a 'threat to the nation's economic efficiency and political stability', what are the implications for the 1990's of such a rate running at a radically higher proportion?

In discussing the themes within which the poverty debate was carried out during the early Rowntree era, Veit Wilson (1986) wrote: "Most middle class people -the class which Rowntree was addressing - believed that the poor had enough money not to live in obvious want and squalor, but instead chose to spend their money on social activities such as drink and gambling. Poverty thus meant a neglect of diet and health, personal appearance and housing. The resulting poor physique and ill-health among the working class were seen as inimical to the production of strong and well-trained workers and soldiers. For the classes who held power and property, the answer to the question of why the poor were poor was critical to their own interests, quite apart from the altruistic concern which some of them, like Rowntree, had for the poor. (pp. 76/7) This sentiment is not really appropriate to today's reality - i.e., that there is no Empire to defend and that many of the unemployed are marginal/surplus/residual to the labour market and are not required to be 'strong and well-trained'. Such a development gives rise to conceptualisations of the 'underclass', marginalisation and residualisation.

In summarising the works of Rowntree, Briggs (1961) explained that, in gathering the information for his analysis, 'he turned neither to socialists nor to social workers, but to physiologists and dieticians'. (p. 32) Similarly, in order to de-politicise the data-collection and calculation processes in this research exercise, the primary poverty line has been drawn by nutritionists, home economists, domestic scientists, textile and energy experts.

Briggs quotes Rowntree as concluding that the poor were no less human than the non-poor, were characterised by the same needs and weaknesses, and differed from the rest of society only in terms of the unjust ways in which they were treated and the unequal demands that society placed upon them: 'Nothing can be gained by closing our eyes to the fact that there is in this country, a large section of the community whose income is insufficient for the purposes of physical efficiency and whose lives are increasingly stunted. If men and women in this class possessed, as a whole, extraordinary energy and perseverance, they might perhaps, notwithstanding physical feebleness and a depressing environment, raise themselves to a higher level; but it is idle to expect from them, as a class, virtues and powers far in excess of those characterising any other section of the community ... These minimum sums assumed not only self-denial, but perfect management, qualities which were, by their nature, rare in working class as in any other families.' (pp. 35/38) In parallel, the minimum estimates put forward here also assume strict discipline and perseverance and income management which a City of London managing director would be proud of, notwithstanding the financial budgeting skills practiced by those who blame the poor for their own difficult predicament.

2 Food

The question of food and nutritional requirements were central and of greatest importance to Rowntree's poverty research. For him, food could be understood under the four headings: (a) the function of food in the body; (b) the quantity necessary; (c) its kind; (d) its cost.

Function

The function of food and its nutrients may therefore be summarised as follows:

Protein forms tissue (muscle, tendon etc. and fat) and serves as fuel	} All yield } energy
Fats form fatty tissue (not muscle etc.) and serves as fuel	} in form of } heat
Carbohydrates are transformed into fat and serve as fuel	} and muscle } strength

Kind of food

The meagre nature of Rowntree's food element in his primary poverty line is featured in the following statement: '... valuable suggestions may be gained from the diets provided for able-bodied paupers in the work-houses, as the object of these institutions is to provide a diet containing the necessary nutrients at the lowest cost compatible with a certain amount of variety'. (p. 98)

Quantity

In introducing the works of his main nutritional advisor, Professor Atwater from America, Rowntree explained that his standards for men with **moderate** muscular work was adopted - i.e., 3,500 calories of energy value and 125 grammes of protein per man per day (no fats or carbohydrates were specified in the nutrient requirements). In selecting this standard, he was mindful of the fact that the section of wage-earners living near his poverty line was composed mainly of labourers, who generally carried out heavy work. He was aware that their wives laboured hard, washing and scrubbing, and children went to work young, both during the school day and afterwards, often helping at home in scrubbing floors, running errands etc. Again, Rowntree reinforced the parsimonious and meagre nature of his dietary: 'The diet adopted as the present standard in the present chapter has been selected from the rations specified in the new regulations (1901), but the cheapest rations only have been chosen, and on this account, no butcher's meat is included in the dietary. The standard here adopted is therefore less generous than that which would be required by the Local Government Board (in the workhouse).' (1901, p. 99) The dietary adopted here thus attempted to adhere as much as possible to the characteristics of Rowntree's estimates and the costings produced represent the lowest estimates ever of the nutritional requirements of a family. In introducing his own equivalence scales, he calculated that an adult female required 80% of the food of an adult male at moderate muscular labour.

Table 2.1
Equivalence scales used by Rowntree for 1899 study

Male		100%
Female		80%
Boy	14 - 16	80%
Girl	14 - 16	80%
Child	10 - 13	60%
Child	6 - 9	50%
Child	2 - 5	40%
Child	<2 yrs	30% (p. 91)

The following list shows the constituents of each of the foodstuffs used by

Rowntree and his nutritionist advisors, taken from Appendix J (pp. 99/102) of his 1901 book:

Ingredients used in various foodstuffs - Rowntree 1901

Broth, veg.	Pint	2oz. fresh vegs.: 1/2oz dripping: 1 pint meat liquor; salt & pepper to taste
Cake, plain	lb.	7.5ozs flour; 2oz sugar; 2oz dripping; 1oz currants; 1/2gill milk; salt to taste; 1/4oz baking powder; sufficient water
Cake, seed	1b.	13oz bread dough; 2oz sugar; 2oz dripping; 1/4oz carraway seeds
Cocoa (adult)	Pint	1/2oz cocoa; 4/10oz sugar; 3fl.oz milk; sufficient water
Cocoa (children)	Pint	" 1/2 pint milk
Coffee (adult)	Pint	4/10oz coffee (20% chicory); 1/2oz sugar; 3fl. oz milk
Coffee (children)	Pint	" 1/2 pint milk.
Dumplings	1b.	11ozs bread dough
Gruel	Pint	2ozs oatmeal; 1/2oz treacle; sufficient water & salt; allspice
Pudding	1b.	8ozs split peas; 1/4oz fat; salt; meat liquor a sufficiency

Potatoes with milk	1b.	10ozs boiled potatoes; 1oz fat; 1oz flour; 1 gill milk; salt to taste
Pint		4ozs oatmeal; water and salt
Pudding		1b. 8ozs flour, 2ozs suet (beef); salt to taste; sufficient water
Tea (adults)	Pint	2/10oz tea; 1/2oz sugar; 2fl. oz milk; water a sufficiency
Tea (children)	Pint	" 1/2 pint milk

(p. 442)

The proportion of protein contained in the diet is shown separately. The fuel value includes that which is yielded by protein:

Table 2.2
Nutrient specifications for 1899 dietary

	Fuel Value (calories)	Protein (grams)
Men	3478	137
Women	2923	115.5
Children 8-16	2634	87.2
Children 3-8	1824	66.0

(p. 102)

Rowntree (1903) replied to predictable criticism from the Charity Organisation Society, a conservative, philanthropic group who firmly believed in the individualist approach to countering poverty, over his dietary. He argued that one of his main nutritional advisors, Dr. Dunlop, had shown that the dietary analysis may have been inaccurate but: ' ... the possibility of error is that the amount of nutriment in the food may be *over-stated* but the inaccuracies are never on the side of *under-statement*.' (p. 21)

Cost of food

In the following extract, Rowntree introduced a current social policy issue - 'the poor pay more' for the basic necessities of life - and he took account of this when calculating the costs of his weekly dietaries, again in pursuit of as much accuracy as possible: 'We should of course, not be justified in basing the cost of this diet upon the contract prices paid by the (workhouse) Guardians. The poor buy their food in small quantities and thus pay a higher price for it ... a series of investigations was made by the writer, regarding the actual cash prices paid for various foodstuffs by the working classes in York. The average of these prices has been adopted in estimating the cost of the standard diet, except in six cases where the articles could be purchased at lower prices at Cooperative Stores in the city. The following is a table of the prices upon which the cost of the standard diet has been estimated. (The price of bread is not given, as in York, it is the custom to make bread at home, so effecting an economy):

Flour @ 1/4d per stone,
New milk @ 11/2d per pint
Skimmed milk @ 3/4d per pint
Oatmeal @ 2d per lb less 5%
Dried peas @ 21/4d per lb less 5%
Bacon @ 6d per lb
Cheese @ 6.5d per lb
Sugar @ 1 3/4d per lb
Potatoes @ 1/2d per lb
Margarine @ 8d per lb less 5%
Butter @ 1s per lb
Biscuits @ 4d per lb
Cocoa @ 1s per lb less 5%
Tea @ 1s.5d per lb
Coffee @ 1s. per lb less 5%
Treacle @ 1 3/4d lb less 5%
Onions 1/2d per lb
Yeast @ 8d per lb
Currants @ 3.5d per lb
Suet @ 8d per lb
(5% deducted for Co-op foods) (p. 104)

The weekly cost of the standard dietary was as follows:

Men	Women	Children 8 - 16	3 - 8	Under 3
3s.3d	2s.9d	2s.7d	2s.1d	2s.1d

Average for adults	Average for children
3s.	2s.3d.

(No dietary was given in the new workhouse regulations for children under three, the doctor ordering diets specially for each child according to circumstances. The cost was reckoned at 2s.1d. per week, as the large proportion of new milk required by young children increased the cost of the maintenance to that of children who were somewhat older) (p. 105)

In a clear message to home economists, consumer experts, nutritionists, as well as social policy-makers, Rowntree argues: 'These prices refer solely to the cost of the food materials; they include none of the necessary expenses connected with cooking. It must also be remembered that, at present, the poor do not possess knowledge which would enable them to select a diet that is at once nutritious and as economical as that which is adopted here as the standard. Moreover, the adoption of such a diet would require considerable changes in established customs and many prejudices which would have to be up-rooted. (A greater knowledge of cooking and more willingness to take trouble in the preparation of food would also be necessary. For instance, more time is required in the preparation of a breakfast of porridge than for one consisting of tea and bread and butter, and such foods as pease pudding, vegetable broth etc. require considerable pains to be devoted to their preparation if they are to be made palatable). It should also be noted that ... this diet does not contain any fresh meat (it has been eliminated on account of cost) ... My aim throughout has been to select a standard diet which gives adequate nutrition at the lowest practical cost. (The writer is aware that prison diets are even less costly than this standard; but they are so extremely stringent as to be punitive in character and would not serve as a basis for a standard diet for the independent poor).' (pp. 105/6) Above Rowntree quite clearly points to the consideration he gave to 'established customs and many prejudices', features which thus have to be taken account of when calculating a contemporary dietary for a heuristic research exercise.

In 'The Human Needs of Labour' (1936), Rowntree again referred to the practical, if heuristic, employment of his measurements: 'Some people imagine that since diets vary infinitely in character, and individuals vary both in the amount of food which they need and in the amount of physical work which they perform from day to day, it is useless to try to estimate the food requirements of a class. But this is not so. Obviously, no hard and fast figure can be laid down representing with mathematical accuracy, the sum which each individual must spend on food; but it is possible with the aid of investigations made by physiologists, to arrive at a figure sufficiently accurate for my present purpose ... to ascertain what sum members of the class of unskilled workers as a whole must spend upon food, if they are to provide adequately for the maintenance of physical efficiency. No doubt, any general figure of this kind would slightly under-estimate the needs of certain individuals and over-estimate those of others; but it would be absurd to call it useless because of this. It might as well be argued that we could not design a standard chair suitable for a public hall because people differ in height and size, or decide upon a standard height for a doorway because when it was built, some very tall people might knock their heads while others could pass through a much lower one. For all kinds of purposes, standards are fixed which are based upon the normal needs of the class of people concerned; and similarly, it is perfectly possible to fix a standard of food requirements.' (pp. 48/9)

According to his nutritional advisors at the time, the essential constituents of which all food consists were: (1) Protein; (2) Fats; (3) Carbohydrates; (4) Mineral Salts; (5) Vitamins; (6) Water. In April 1933, the British Medical Association (BMA) set up a committee whose terms of reference were: 'To determine the weekly minimum expenditure on foodstuffs which must be incurred by families of various sizes if health and working capacity are to be maintained and to construct specimen diets ... The Committee ... recommends the adoption of the figure 3,400 cals. in the food as purchased as the unit requirement of the normal man of average stature, if health and working capacity are to be maintained.' (1936, pp. 57/9) Rowntree noted that the standard laid down by the B.M.A. was for 'moderate' work. He cast doubt on whether the work normally done by the class of workers he was investigating should have been classed as 'light', 'moderate' or 'heavy'. On reviewing the world of unskilled labour, he believed that, in placing it halfway, as regards severity, between light work and heavy work, he was erring on the side of moderation. To adopt a lower estimate would have involved an underestimation of the claims of physical efficiency. This research has gone beyond even Rowntree's concessions in adopting low activity levels of the subjects for the purposes of constructing a dietary, by placing such levels at an almost totally sedentary lifestyle.

Using the works of Cathcart and Murray of 1931, which were adopted by the B.M.A.s 1936 report, Rowntree was able to tabulate the food requirements of women and children, viz-a-viz those of adult men (mean value).

Table 2.3
Equivalence scales used in 1936 study

An adult female requires	0.83 of an adult male
A boy of 14 or over needs	1.00 "
A girl of 14 or over needs	0.83 "
A child of 12-14	0.90 "
A child of 10-12	0.80 "
A child of 8-10	0.70 "
A child of 6- 8	0.60 "
A child of 3- 6	0.50 "
A child of 2- 3	0.40 "
A child of 1- 2	0.30 "
A child of 0- 1	0.20 "

Rowntree thus proposed to take as the average equivalent for each child, 0.65 of an adult man and in doing so, he believed that he was not over-stating the needs of women and children by basing the food requirements of the whole family, as the Committee of the B.M.A. had done, on those of men engaged in moderate work. **Stressing the important significance of advances in the science of nutrition and dietetics** to calculations such as his own and to other social research, Rowntree wrote: 'Had I been writing on the subject of food requirements 20 years ago, I could have concluded that what I had to say at this point, but within recent years, a great deal of research has been done on dietetics and important discoveries have been made. It has been found that health and vigour depend on the presence in the diet of certain mineral salts and of vitamins.' (p. 66) Again any attempt at adopting Rowntree's approaches must consider the advances achieved, in this case, in the scientific progress in the area of nutrition. In concluding his nutritional calculations, he adopted the following standards as representing the amount of food necessary for unskilled workers and their families:

Table 2.4
Nutrient specifications for 1936 dietary

	Protein (grams)	Fuel energy (cals)
Men	100	3400
Women	83	2820
Children (under 14)	65	2210

He added that half the protein should be first class or animal protein. The diet should also contain an adequate quantity of 'protective food'. (p. 70) Again, referring to the contributions of nutritional research, this time in helping to formulate equivalence scales for food needs, he explained that research had suggested raising the coefficients for expressing the requirements of women and children in terms of 'man-values'. That for a woman was only raised slightly - from 0.8 to 0.83 - but those for children were raised fairly considerably. In Chapter III (Dietary), he translated the nutriment body into a dietary: ' ... the choice of a dietary should be guided by considerations of the greatest possible economy commensurate with due regard to national customs ... In this country, almost everyone takes a mixed diet - even the poorest try to get a certain amount of meat; and though undoubtedly, health can be maintained without it, we cannot, in selecting our dietary, ignore the fact that meat-eating is a universal custom ... we may reasonably exclude alcoholic beverages, but should bear in mind possible expenditure upon them when considering the amount to be allowed for personal sundries.' (pp. 78/9) Above, Rowntree again mentions consideration of 'national customs' such as meat eating and a 'mixed diet'. The dietary adopted here has thus tried to establish a balance between permitting only 'the greatest possible economy' and very modest customary eating habits. Lest anyone should have continued to misunderstand the nature and meaning of Rowntree's exercises, he repeated: 'I have selected a dietary on which to base the standard of living. It certainly cannot be called extravagant; it errs, if at all, on the side of undue economy. Indeed, I should like to make it clear that I do not put it forward as the kind of dietary that I consider entirely satisfactory for unskilled workers. I do so rather as representing a standard below which, no class of worker should be forced to live...' (p.79) Similarly, we do not present our dietary as a prescription for nutritional standards but purely as a floor below which no family should be expected to thrive or enjoy physical efficiency and adherence to customary eating habits.

In a final whittling down of his nutritional estimates, Rowntree addressed the issue of fresh milk and explained that the B.M.A. in its dietary allowed for 14 pints of fresh milk per week for a family of five; but, on the grounds that fresh skimmed milk, which was largely consumed by the lower paid workers 20 years previous, could not easily be bought in 1936, he therefore provided for the purchase of tinned milk only. (p. 85)

Commencing his 'Poverty and the Welfare State' works with Laver, they explained that they adopted the same dietary as in 1936, except for small modifications which it was necessary to make and which did not materially affect the total nutritive value of the dietary. For example, they substituted white flour for wholemeal flour, since the former was heavily subsidised and the latter was not. It required about 23.5lb. of white flour to provide the calories contained in 16.5lb. of wholemeal flour, and so they included this amount in the dietary. They also assumed that bread was bought from the baker instead of being baked at home, since this was not practicable in many 1940/50's stoves. And, as fresh milk was heavily subsidised and condensed milk was not, they substituted 14 pints of fresh milk for 12 tins of skimmed condensed milk. (p. 9) Taking consideration of the fact that school children received 1/3 pint of milk a day during approximately 180 days a year, which was equal to 1/6 pint throughout the year, the following table reflected the effect of the changes between the 1936 and 1950 dietaries:

Deduct from 1936 diet (grammes)	**Calories**	**Protein**
Replacement of skimmed condensed milk by fresh full cream milk	3010	28.0
Cheese 6 ozs	702	42.6
Bacon (streaky) 4 ozs	516	8.8
Dripping & Suet 10 ozs	2530	-
	6758	79.4
Add to 1936 dietary		
School milk for 3 children, 3.5d pints	1190	63.0
Margarine 16 ozs	3480	-
Sugar 18 ozs	1944	-
	6622	63.0

As the total number of calories in the diet was nearly 80,000 and the amount of protein over 2,400 grammes, it can be seen that the effect of the modifications of the diet which had been made were quite insubstantial. (pp. 9/10) This dietary provided for a family with three children under the age of 14, the quantity of calories and the amount of protein deemed as adequate by the 1933 B.M.A. Committee. (p. 10) The nutritional requirements of the adult male were calculated on the basis that he was engaged in 'work of modern severity'. It also provided the calories and the protein for adult females and children according to the standards laid down by the B.M.A. Committee. A Miss Schulz of Oxford University's Institute of Statistics calculated the calories, protein, mineral salts and vitamins in the dietary as amended. Based on this information, the following table was the dietary adopted:

Breast of mutton (imported) 2½lb @ 8d lb	1/8
Minced beef 2lb @ 1/4 per lb	2/8

Shin of beef 1.5lb @ 1/6 per lb	2/3
Liver - 1lb @ 1/6 per lb	1/6
Beef sausages - 1lb @ 1/3 per lb	1/3
Bacon 1 1/4 lb @ 1/11d. per lb (cheapest cut)	2/4 3/4
Cheese 10ozs @ 1/2 per lb	-/8 3/4
Fresh full cream milk - 14 pints @ 5d pint	5/10
Herrings 1.5d lb @ 8d per lb	1/-
Kippers 1lb @ 1s per lb	1/-
Sugar - 3 lb 2oz : 5d per lb	1/3½d
Potatoes - 14lb @ 9lb for	1/6½d
23.5lb of bread - 13.5 loaves @ 5½d each	6/2 1/4
Oatmeal - 2lb @ 6d per lb	1/-
Margarine 2.5lb @ 10d per lb	2/1
Cooking fat - 10ozs @ 1s per lb	7½d
Flour - 1 1/4 lb @ 9.5d per 3lb bag	-/4
Jam - 1lb @ 1/2 per lb	1/2
Treacle - 1lb @ 10d (in tin)	-/10
Cocoa - 1/4lb @ 8.5d per 1/4lb	-8½d
Rice - 10ozs @ 9d per lb	-5½d
Sago - 1/4lb @ 9d per lb	-/2 1/4
Barley - 2ozs @ 9d per lb	-/1
Peas - 1/2lb @ 10.5d per lb	- 5 1/4
Lentils - 3/4lb @ 10.5d per lb	-/8
Stoned dates - 1/2lb @ 10.5d per lb	-/5 1/4
Swedes - 6lb @ 2.5d per lb	1/3
Onions - 4.5lb @ 5d per lb	1/10 1/2
Apples - 4lb @ 5d per lb	1/8
Egg - 1 @ 3.5d	-/3 1/2
Extra vegetables & fruit	1/6
Tea - 1/2lb @ 3/4 per lb	1/8
Extras, including salt, seasoning etc.	-/9
TOTAL (for man, woman + 3 children under 14)	**47s./4d.**

(This dietary was drawn up in the early part of October 1950. The prices of the different items were based on information gathered by an investigator who visited a number of shops which catered for working class people). (pp. 12/13)

Again using the food equivalence scales of Cathcart and Murray, Rowntree established that an adult female required 83% as much food as an adult male, and the requirements of the children varied according to age and sex. The dietary for a family of five thus had a 'mean value' of 3.78.

In calculating the necessary expenditure on food, they allowed 12s./6d. for a man, 10s./5d. for a woman and 8s./1d. for each child.

In 1933 the BMA set up a committee whose brief was, 'to determine the minimum weekly expenditure on foodstuffs which must be incurred by families of varying size if health and working capacity are to be maintained and to construct specimen diets'. Rowntree used the standards laid down by this committee for his 1936 dietary (Rowntree 1936, pp.51-56). It varied in that the calorific values were less; 3,400 (adult male) as opposed to the 3,500 that he had specified in his 1899 study. The protein content was also reduced to 100g., of which 50g. was to be first-class protein. Animal fat (100g.) was also included, as was an addition of 500g. of carbohydrate. Rowntree used the measurement of 'moderate' work to calculate his energy requirements, as opposed to heavy work which many of the inhabitants of York were engaged in. The BMA used Cathcart and Murray's methods of assessing the requirements for women and children and Rowntree used this method once again in 1936.

As a result of his expertize in establishing budget standards he was appointed as an advisor to Beveridge during the planning stages of the welfare state in 1942, when the cost of a dietary **was** specified. It has been extremely difficult to substantiate what post-war governments based their National Assistance, Supplementary Benefit (see Stitt 1989) and Income Support rates on for food budgets (or any other component of family budgets). This exercise hopes to throw some light on the possible costs of a subsistence diet in 1992 (albeit lacking in variety), based on the concept adopted by Rowntree of producing an irreducible budget for food which would achieve physical efficiency, as well as counteract the critics who believe that the poor are well provided for, but they just spend their incomes unwisely.

The dietary that has been devised in 1992 takes into account the many changes that have evolved since the Rowntree studies, as indeed, Rowntree continuously took account of the progress made in nutritional science, evolution of national customs and other considerations. Food storage and preservation techniques have expanded the range and types of foods now available. Over 98% of the population now have either a refrigerator or freezer thus enabling more 'fresh' food to be bought and stored. Less than half of all households with incomes between £100 and £125 own a car, which will be seen as an important factor when food shopping. (CSO 1991) Freezers now occupy more floor space in supermarkets than ever before. There are now a vast array of convenience foods from which to choose. As would be expected, to devise a budget using such foods would fuel criticism which Rowntree had sought to abate for reasons stated. Firstly the food budget should fulfil nutritional adequacy (defined by official guidelines), at the most economical cost and the dietary should be palatable and adhere to current social customs. If these convenience foods were chosen, it would require more in the way of energy requirements in order to fulfil the vitamin and mineral content and the dietary would be much more expensive, thus inviting reasonable criticism. Each household has its own preferences and it would be impossible to accommodate all these needs within the remit of this study. Complete disregard could not be realistically made against including such foods, so a small amount of ready prepared foods was included.

Households face ever increasing choices of convenience foods to consume, generally the foods being more expensive than those produced at home from the basic ingredients. It was decided to combine traditionally prepared foods with the lower priced convenience foods. Rowntree himself pondered on just how long a woman could spend in the kitchen, and he also remarked on the skill and ingenuity required by such women in managing the household budget (Rowntree, p. 29). It would be unfair of this study to imply that women or men should return to spending hours in the kitchen when faced with the vast variety of convenience foods now available. The 1992 dietary did allow for a small percentage of convenience food (i.e., tinned baked beans and frozen fish fingers) which are quite basic when compared to the more up-market meals which now pack out the freezers in supermarkets. In addition to the latter, traditionally prepared foods made up the majority of the menus. All the foods were chosen for their valuable nutritional contribution to the dietary and their current low cost.

It is acknowledged that there are many different ways of constructing a dietary using a variety of different foods. The dietary should stand up to three basic criteria: is it realistic and does it bear any resemblance to current eating habits; secondly, would the diet be acceptable, not just for one person for one week, but for a number of persons over a period of time; finally, does it assume perfect conditions - i.e., does the consumer have access to all the necessary materials and is there a small stock of staples included within the budget? (Leather 92) In addressing the three points in turn, the dietary does fulfil the criteria, but with reservations.

Is it realistic? The immediate answer to this question would be yes, as it was compiled with information obtained from the National Food Survey (NFS); however some basic foodstuffs, like bread, would require an increase in consumption per head to adhere to the diet specified and this would be in direct contradiction of the downward trends in the consumption of bread, cereal products and potatoes since the 1950s. The NFS also reveals that the diet of the nation does not comply with the Dietary Reference Values (DRVs.

DoH 1991), whereas the foods and amounts chosen for this dietary do adhere to these official standards, (MAFF 1992, NFS 1990) in the same way that Rowntree's 1936 dietary adhered to the BMA's 1933 guidelines. The dietary was not constructed as a model for prescription, nor was it advocating increases in consumption of these staple foods; it only sought to inform that a nutritious minimum budget standard for food could be achieved by changing the amounts of certain familiar foods consumed. In changing the amounts of food, would this make the diet unacceptable? Obviously, this question could not be answered without extensive testing. The multi-faceted concept of an acceptable diet make the question one which is impossible to answer. If we take the satiety value of food, the diet may not be acceptable to those with either large or small appetites, as the diet would be largely controlled by the food portion sizes within the MAFF publication (Crawley, MAFF). The diet does not take into account personal preferences, wants or needs and does not fulfil all tastes, concentrating only on the basic types of foodstuffs. The diet was directed only at one section of the population, families with children, and did not cater for ethnic or cultural variances;

Would the diet be acceptable for a longer period? Presumably this question implies that the lack of variety would not be acceptable. To a large extent this would be true but during the course of the investigations, it became apparent that many families could only purchase foods which were both tried and tested. They could not afford to make mistakes, as food not eaten has no nutritional value and a back-up stock is rare. During an interview with one mother in her home, she apologised for not offering a cup of tea as she had none left, all she had was three cheap tins of peas in the cupboard until she received her benefit the next day. Straying from the acceptable can also be costly. In an effort to cut down on her fat intake, one woman's response was to stop purchasing her normal margarine and try a low fat spread; but the family would not eat it, even though the healthier alternative had cost more and she had to dispose of it. Although not within the remit of this study, it is important to note that advise about fat is considerably confusing, and often results in abandonment of efforts. What is clearly needed is a national food policy which seeks to make healthier alternative more economically attractive in order to help people change their diets.

For one family, the reality of no choice meant that a sack of potatoes and a tray of eggs provided the only foods for the evening meals, the only option available was whether to have 'egg and chips or chips and egg'. The children from this family were aware that they were not eating healthily and had asked their mother why she never bought any fruit? Lack of control over their financial situation and her obvious feelings of despair were apparent. Data from the NFS have shown that higher income groups consume more fruit and vegetables than the lower income groups, clearly due to factors such as price and availability, and it is generally these foods that are the first to be omitted from the diet when money is fixed at a low level. The National Children's Homes (NCH) survey (1992) found that 68% of those families with children living on benefit said that they did not have enough money to buy food and also that they had missed meals due to lack of money. (p. 20) Ideally the dietary should have a healthy variety of foods, but for the purposes of determining a minimum food budget, variety has been superseded by the need to adhere to Rowntree's premise, to provide for 'physical efficiency only', and, with apologies, errs on the side of 'undue economy'. There would appear to be no element of choice, 'people are simply in a position where essential needs vie with one another,'(Leather 1992, p.3), and with healthy food costing more than the unhealthy alternatives it leaves no room for manoeuvre in low income families, resulting in poor diets and poor health.

Finally does the dietary assume perfect conditions? For the purposes of this study, certain assumptions were made on the ownership of refrigerators and knowledge of basic cooking skills and access to cooking equipment and utensils. The family would ideally have a refrigerator with a small freezing compartment. When the oven was in use, full utilisation should be made of it to prepare other foods - i.e., when roasting a chicken, baked potatoes, scones or rice pudding could also be prepared; maximum use is then made of the fuel consumed. Some foods which could be prepared at home were found to be more cost effective, but less time consuming if bought ready made, as is the case with yogurts, which have steadily increased in popularity over the years. The making of home-made yogurts is not a common practice and requires a heat source and flask, thus raising the cost and effort, as opposed to purchasing ready-made. Rowntree had updated his ideas on acceptable purchases from his initial survey where he included the ingredients for making bread, to the later versions which included the cost of ready made loaves.

The study assumed easy access to the local discount food retail outlets; the study also assumed access to local markets for the purchase of fruit and vegetables. Obviously these assumptions would not hold true for all households, and in making such presumptions, the study acknowledges that it errs on the side of an underestimation of cost and accessibility in all areas. For example, if a household has to rely on local corner shops for their foods, this will inevitably increase the amount of money spent, as small shops cannot compete with the large multiples for price or variety. Similarly the lack of access to a local market can make the purchase of fruit and vegetables prohibitive for low income families.

The 1992 primary food poverty line needed to provided for physical efficiency using the current nutritional guidelines as set out in the DRVs and with consideration of the contents of the 1984 National Advisory Council on Nutrition Education (NACNE) report. Rowntree had based his energy content on the 'moderately active' level, even though he was aware that the families he observed led very hard lives, requiring long hours of laborious work. Men's work was heavy manual labour whilst women spent long hours 'washing and scrubbing', and even the children were expected to work to help out financially. Estimates of energy requirements have reduced since Rowntree's observations, from 3,500 Kcalories for a male in 1899 to 2,500 Kcalories in 1992. So too has the basis of assessing energy needs changed. In 1899 Rowntree based his estimations of the energy required on a moderately active lifestyle, whilst in 1992 they were based on a Personal Activity Level (PAL) of 1.4. The Dietary Reference Values (DRVs) introduced the new concept of PARs (Personal Activity Ratios), which replaced the previous categories of sedentary, moderately active and very active which were the basis for calculation of energy requirements. Rowntree had based his calculations on a 'moderately active lifestyle' with which to determine the energy needs of his family. This was, as Rowntree pointed out, an underestimation of the needs of his families. Rowntree had used the work of Cathcart and Murray, to devise equivalence scales with which to calculate the needs of various family members based on age. This somewhat crude method is obviously now superseded by more scientific measurements of need. The PAL of 1.4 for the adult male and female diets is recommended, which in simple terms, equates with an inactive lifestyle. The DRVs inform us that, 'due to the inactive lifestyles of much of the population, a PAL of 1.4 should be assumed in the absence of other information on activity'. (DoH, DRVs, p.25) The PAL can be determined by the following equation:

Daily energy expenditure = BMR x (time in bed + time at work x PAR) + (non-occupational time x PAR)

PAR = Physical Activity Ratio

BMR = Basal Metabolic Rate

In this important way, the basis of the dietaries calculated here is even lower, relatively, than Rowntree's, who founded his estimates on a moderately active lifestyle and thus the under-estimations referred to by him are magnified in this study. The recommendations for children were based on the estimated average intakes of children aged 3 - 10 years. There was suggestion by the World Health Organisation, among others, that the intakes of children should be increased by 5% to allow for 'a desirable level of physical activity'. Concerns were expressed by the research team that if the increases were incorporated into the recommendations, the extra energy may result in the development of obesity and so we declined to take this course of action. In the case of children, the energy levels were based on estimated average requirements, (EARs). As with most nutrients, the energy levels were higher for males than females. For ease of calculation, an average was taken of the two values for girls and boys in each age category for four to six years, and seven to ten years:

Table 2.5
Estimated daily requirements for energy, 1992

	Male	Female	Child	Child	Total
Age	19-49	19-49	4-6	7-10	
Energy					
Kcal	2550	1940	1630	1855	7975

The diet was constructed and evaluated with the use of the Microdiet programme installed at John Moores' University. The first requirement was to adhere to the Reference Nutrient Intake (RNI) recommendations with regard to the four main nutrients - Protein, Fat, Carbohydrate, and Non-Starch-Polysaccharides - whilst ensuring that the mineral and nutrient content also reached adequate levels as specified in the DRVs.

The DRVs recognise that the typical UK diet currently comprises 15% of the energy value taken as protein and on this basis, this study has elected to use the percentage of 15% of energy intake on which to base its protein component.

Table 2.6
Estimated daily requirements of protein, 1992
(Based on 15% of energy intake)

Table	Male	Female	Child	Child	Total
Age	19-49	19-49	4-6	7-10	
Protein	95.6	72.4	61.1	69.6	299

The following example illustrates how the protein element of the diet was calculated using the male energy requirement as the reference point:

1 gram dietary protein provides 4 Kcal or 17 kJ
15% of 2550 Kcals = 382.5 Kcals

$$\frac{382.5 \text{ Kcal}}{4} = 96 \text{ grams protein daily}$$

Carbohydrate comprises of non-milk extrinsic sugars and intrinsic and milk sugars and starch. Carbohydrates are extremely important in that they provide a large percentage of the energy required by man for physical efficiency. Intrinsic sugars are found within the cellular structure of foods. Extrinsic sugars are, as their name suggests, found outside the structures of foods - i.e., honey or in their refined form as table sugar. It is the extrinsic sugars that have caused concern, for they are known to be a major cause of dental caries in the UK. The DRVs for total carbohydrates estimate that approximately 50% of total energy should be derived from carbohydrates, with intrinsic and milk sugars and starches accounting for the 39%, and non-milk extrinsic sugars (mainly sucrose) making up no more than 11% of the total carbohydrate content:

Table 2.7
Estimated daily requirement of carbohydrate, 1992

	Male	Female	Child	Child	Total
Age	19-49	19-49	4-6	7-10	
CHO	340	259	217	247	1063

The NACNE report of 1983 set long term goals for the year 2000 which advised that the fat content of the diet should be reduced to approximately 30% of the total energy. The DRVs set a slightly higher measurement for fat at 33% (35% diet, excluding alcohol). The DRV for saturated fats was set at 10% (11% diet, excluding alcohol) with polyunsaturated fats at 6% (6.5% with the exclusion of alcohol), and mono-unsaturated fat at 12% (13% excluding alcohol). It is now ten years since the recommendations of the NACNE report, but there would appear to be very little improvement in fat consumption levels. Across all income groups and family types, the data suggests that fat intake was running at approximately 40-42% in 1990. The saturated fat content is also much higher than the current DRVs which in 1990 constituted 16.6% compared to the 1992 DRVs of 11%, although it is true to say that saturated fat in the diet has decreased since 1970.

It has been found that diets which are low in non-starch-polysaccharides (NSP) are generally those which are found to be high in fat and sugar. NSP is the term used in the DRVs which has superseded the old term of 'dietary fibre' used by both NACNE the RDAs. This term was abandoned by the COMA panel in favour of the more scientifically correct term, NSP. NSPs are less energy dense and provide good satiety value, which can be both beneficial in prevention and treatment of obesity. At present the average intakes in the UK are between 5g. and 25g. daily. In view of the association of bowel disorders with low consumption of NSPs, and in pursuit of Rowntree's 'physical efficiency' ethos, the research team set the dietary reference value for NSPs at an average of 18g. daily, with children above the age of two scaled down accordingly. No recommendations were set for children under the age of two. Table 2.8 was devised for the moderate family of two adults and two children from the DRVs and also combining the main themes of the NACNE report.

With the aid of Microdiet, a computer food analysis package installed at the John Moores' University, Liverpool, a series of menus were drawn up, and analyses of the nutrient content of the food were obtained.

Table 2.8
Estimated daily nutrient requirements of 'moderate family'

	Male	Female	Child 4-6	Child 7-10	Total
Energy Kcal	2550	1940	1630	1855	7975
Protein grams	96	73	61	70	300
Fat grams	99	76	63	72	310
CHO grams	340	259	217	247	1063
NSP grams	18	14	11	13	56
Vit C mg	40	40	30	30	140
Calcium mg	700	600	500	500	2300
Iron mg	8.7	14.8	6.1	8.7	38.3
Thiamin mg	1	0.8	0.7	0.7	3.2

MAFF's own guidelines regarding food portion sizes were used to construct the menus. However, the use of this method does not take into account any variation of appetite or individual preferences. Some modifications to food portion sizes were made in order to comply with the estimated requirements. No allowances were made for any food wastage (the NFS suggests 10% wastage), only a very small stock of staples were included in the food list which included: flour for home baking, cooking oil, etc. In addition to the menu plans, a few foods were included to provide what can only be described as a meagre 'treat' - i.e., one packet of digestive biscuits, one packet of crisps each and one half bottle of undiluted fruit juice per week. The main food items were costed at Kwik-Save supermarket and at local street markets for fruit and vegetables:

Shopping List

Cornflakes	.81
Skimmed milk 10pts	1.97
Wholemeal bread *8 @ 800g	4.72
Margarine 500g	.38
Cheddar Cheese @£1.55/lb	2.32
Low fat Frutti yogurt 67p for 6	1.38
Tuna 2 cans @ 39p	.78
Mushrooms ½lb	.50
Pasta (Lasagne)	.58
Bananas @ 39p/lb	.78
Cocoa	.65
Mandarin oranges tinned 312g	.35
Shredded wheat (18) 96p	.48
Orange juice 2 cartons	1.38
Soft baps (6)	.55
Beefburgers (pkt 10) 97p	.58
Baked beans 5*425g	1.15
Minced beef @1.69/lb	1.26
Onions @10p/lb	.15
Carrots @10p/lb	.20
Turnip @10p/lb	.15
Leek @40p/lb	.40
Potatoes @35p/5lb	.53
Apples @39p/lb	.97
Lambs liver @69p/lb	.69
Cornflour 35p/8wks	.04
Oxo (12) 52p/3wks	.17

Eggs size 4 1 dozen	.89
Tomatoes tinned 3 @ 19p	.57
Pasta shells	.58
Courgettes 50p/lb	.25
Vegetable soup 2 tins	.76
Weetabix (24)/2wks	.40
Coffee 100g @1.59/2Wks	.79
Pizza 425g @	.79
Salad (mixed salad vegetables)	1.00
Cauliflower	.49
Cheese sauce mix	.34
Fish fingers (10) @ 1.05	.84
Oven chips 49p/2lb	.49
Garden peas tinned	.27
Chicken 3lb wt	1.95
Cabbage @15p/lb	.30
Pineapples tinned 425g	.32
Pkt pearl barley 34p/10wks	.03
Self raising flour 1.5 Kg/6wks	.06
Dried fruit /6wks	.10
Tea mantunna (80s)	.79
Sugar 1kg/2wks	.26
Sunflower oil /6wks	.09
Sub total	36.21

Extras

Condiments		.25
Orange juice 79p/2wks		.40
Digestive biscuits 300g		.51
Potato crisps * 4 @13p		.52
Unexpected needs		2.00
Sub total		3.68
8% Meals = free school dinners		-2.63
	Total	**£37.26**

Using the aforementioned foods, menus were constructed for one week for a family of two adults and two children:

Sunday

Breakfast
Poached egg on wholemeal toast
Fruit juice
Margarine/marmalade
Tea/Coffee

Lunch
Roast chicken, roast potatoes
cabbage, carrot & turnip,
rice pudding

Evening Meal
Vegetable soup
Cheeseburgers and baked beans
bananas.

Supper (everyday)
Cocoa/Tea/Coffee
Wholemeal bread

Monday

Breakfast
Shredded wheat
Skimmed milk
Wholemeal toast
Tea/Coffee

Lunch
Home made chicken
broth, wholemeal bread,
scones

Evening meal
Tuna in bolognese sauce
Pasta, wholemeal bread

Tuesday

Breakfast
Cornflakes
Skimmed milk
Toasted wholemeal bread

Lunch
Beans on wholemeal toast
Grated cheese
Tomatoes

Evening meal
Liver and onion casserole
Jacket potatoes
carrot turnip, gravy

Wednesday

Breakfast
Cornflakes
Skimmed milk
Toasted wholemeal bread

Lunch
Welsh rarebit
Low fat yogurt
Wholemeal bread

Evening meal
Vegetable and beef stew
Stewed apples
Wholemeal bread

Thursday

Breakfast
Weetabix, skimmed milk
Toasted wholemeal bread
Marmalade, margarine

Lunch
Cheese and tomato pizza
Mixed salad, mandarin oranges

Evening meal
Cauliflower cheese, jacket potatoes
Scones

Friday

Breakfast
Cornflakes, skimmed milk
Toasted wholemeal bread
marmalade, margarine

Lunch
Scrambled eggs on toast
Chopped tomatoes, pineapples in fruit juice

Evening meal
Vegetable lasagne
Low fat yogurt

Saturday

Breakfast
Cornflakes, skimmed milk
Toasted wholemeal bread
Margarine, marmalade

Lunch
Grilled fish fingers
Oven chips
Garden peas
Scones

Evening meal
Baked potatoes, grated cheese
Mixed salad, bananas, custard

Analysis of the nutrients available from the weekly menu plan for the 'moderate family' are shown in the next table:

Table 2.9
Nutrient content of 1992 dietary

Kilocalorie		7881	
Kilojoules		33231	
Protein	g	320	16% total energy
Fat	g	286	32% total energy
Saturated Fat	g	88	10% total enery
Mono+Poly unsaturated		150	
CHO	g	1076	51% total energy
Fibre	g	21	
NSP	g	18	
Alcohol	g	0	
Extrinsic Sugars	g	19	
Intrinsic Sugars	g	72	
Calcium	mg	3716	

Selected Vitamins an Minerals

Iron	mg	63.5
Vitamin C	mg	308.5
Thiamin (B1)	mg	7

Intakes (of vitamins and minerals) are generally likely to be far greater than requirements. A variable proportion is actually absorbed into the body (5-10% Iron). The amount absorbed normally balances the amount lost in urine and sweat. (Manual of Nutrition 1989, p. 34)

It should be stressed that the foods chosen were not universally the most economical available, neither were they the most expensive; a certain amount of subjectivity was used by the home economists to ensure that the best overall value was obtained in terms of price and nutrient content. An example would be that some tins of beans can contain a higher percentage of tomato sauce than others which would lower the nutritional value available to the family. At present most of the foods available in the UK are required to specify their ingredients, with some manufacturers taking this one step further and giving a percentage and nutritional breakdown. This enables customers to make more informed choices. If the example of a tin of beans is used and the customer knew that 10% was tomato sauce in one brand and only 5% in another, this may influence decision to purchase.

Items such as tea and coffee and other familiar foods such as cornflakes used the costings of well known brands. By making the decision to use a certain amount of brand names, the choice of food outlets at which the costing could be carried out was reduced, due to many of the newer discount outlets carrying a large percentage of virtually unknown brands. These brands may be comparable with the known brands in price but may not be in nutrient content. The team felt that choosing unfamiliar foods would not be in keeping with one of Rowntree's stipulations, that of being a palatable diet which did not deviate from the social customs of the day.

Would the store chosen for the costings be accessible for the families? There are a number of large multiple food retailers in Liverpool and some food discount stores. The large multiples such as ASDA, TESCO and Sainsbury's are generally located near to good road and motorway networks. It has been suggested that this is a form of social deprivation for those families who do not have access to cars. The opportunity to bulk buy is effectively denied to those on low incomes as lugging home a heavy shopping trolley needs extra money for bulk purchases and a means of getting home either by public transport, or car, an impossible task for young mothers with children in tow. Research has also shown that if similar baskets of goods priced in the multiples and at Kwik-Save are compared, that Kwik-Save's basket was 5% less than the multiples on price. (NCC, p.106) Another point in favour of Kwik-Save is their policy of locating their shops within communities, thereby making economic shopping accessible to the local community. The logical choice for this study was to use Kwik-Save based on the economic costings and accessibility. By costing both in Kwik-Save and in local markets for fruit and vegetables, the study realises that it was again assuming ideal conditions of access, when this is obviously not the case, as many households do not have the luxury of either facility and are forced to rely on smaller shops who cannot compete with the bigger organisations on price or variety. This would mean that the shopping basket may indeed cost more than the price put forward here. The items were costed at the Stonedale Kwik-Save store in Liverpool district 11 in October 1992. The fruit and vegetables were priced in Kirkby Market and Coleman's fruit and vegetable stores. As with all seasonal produce the prices will fluctuate; these particular vegetables were chosen for their economy and availability at the time of the study.

The weekly food budget for 1992 using the Rowntree method came to £39.89. If the provision for free school meals is deducted from the estimated cost this gives a true cost for the family whose children are in receipt of these meals. Approximately 8% of all the families meals are taken through the free school meal; this equates with £2.63 weekly, giving a total of £37.26 for a subsistence, primary food budget. If the above figure is compared with current data on the expenditure of similar family types and income groups and compared also with estimates from various quarters on the costs of a healthy diet, important differences can be found. The Family Spending survey found that families of the same composition as our model family spent on average £64.03 per week on food which equates with an extra £7 daily for each family member. The lowest weekly income band specified for this type of family was £275 and under and they are estimated to spend an average of £46.82 a week on food. Firstly, the higher end of the income band has more than double the income of the same family type who live on Income Support of £105 weekly, therefore, families at the lower end of this income band would obviously be unable to afford to spend this amount on food:

Table 2.10
Comparison of food expenditure by household type & income group

(Family Spending 1991)

Income	£275<	£275-375	£375-500	£550
2 Adults+ Children	£64.03	£58.52	£64.49	£81.05
Income	£100-125	£150-175	£175-225	£225-275
All H/holds	£31.01	£33.08	£38.16	£41.67

The table shows quite clearly that there is a difference of approximately £22 between food expenditure of families with two adults and two children with incomes below £275 and all households groups with incomes below £275.

The Family Budget Unit estimated a 'low cost' food budget amounting to £53.15 for a family of two adults and two children, £16 higher a week that adopted here; clearly household with incomes below £275 are not achieving this level of expenditure on food. In an exercise undertaken by MAFF to determine the low cost of a healthy diet they estimated that this could be achieved for £10.00 per person weekly, or £40 per week for the family. The MAFF dietary, when disaggregated into daily amounts of various foodstuffs involves:

1/4 slice of processed cheese;
less than an edible portion of one chicken wing;
less than a rasher of streaky bacon;
less than half the fish in one fish finger;
less than one egg **per week**;
less than 1/3 of a pint of whole milk;
less than 1/5 of a pint of skimmed milk;
1 medium sized baked potato;
1 table spoonful of baked beans;
1 table spoonful of sweetcorn;
1/10 of an average glass of fruit juice;
less than 1/5 of an average portion of tinned fruit salad;
1 rich tea biscuit etc.

Observers have noted that, to conform to the MAFF low cost healthy diet, low income households would have to cut out meat consumption almost entirely, more than double their consumption of tinned fruit and frozen vegetables (they cannot afford fresh fruit and vegetables), more than double their consumption of breakfast cereals (to obtain the required levels of fibre and fortified vitamins), eat five times more wholemeal bread than at present and eat more white bread. Of the eight slices of bread to be eaten each day, only three would have even a thin spread of margarine or butter - the rest would have to be eaten dry. Yoghurts and other dairy products are completely ruled out. (NCC 1992, Chapter 6) The fact that this almost inhuman, certainly drab and meagre, diet costs £40 per week, whilst the dietary adopted in this research costs £37.26, reinforces the subsistence, low cost and minimal nature of the food budget standard adopted here. This study puts forward the low estimate of £37.26 not as a prescriptive dietary nor as a model for usage, but as an irreducible minimum which only verifies the subsistence nature of the dietary. To summarise, this dietary does not allow for any wastage, all food purchased must be consumed, there are no allowances built into the budget for a standby meal, only £2.00 is allowed for any extras or snacks for visitors, the budget allows for only a very meagre stock of foods remaining at the end of the week.

It is common knowledge that the average UK diet does not adhere to the DRVs. Families interviewed for this study spoke of times when they simply ran out of food, and it was generally women who subjugated their own nutritional needs to those of their families. Various methods were found to be used by families to tide themselves over until the next income was due. Mothers cited going without meals, or just having tea and toast. One mother told of how she could only afford to buy one piece of braising steak for her husband whilst she and the children had sausages. She lamented on the fact that the oven was on for hours for one piece of steak. Borrowing from relatives for the purchase of food was common. One couple could not conceive what their living conditions would be like if it were not for the help afforded by this couple's parents, in the form of weekly food parcels. It was not unusual for families in receipt of milk tokens to be able to cash them in for food at the local shop, often the purchases would cost them more than if they paid cash -another instance of the poor paying more. Concern has been expressed by the British Dietetic Association (BDA) over the problems associated with inadequate income, which precludes people from making the often more expensive choice of healthier foods. Other surveys have found similar problems concerning the deficiency of nutrients among women. A report on nutritional deficiencies amongst UK adults found that for fibre, the intake of 75% of women and 94% of men was below the 30mg. per day recommended by NACNE; other deficiencies included vitamin C, vitamin D and iron. (Jenkins 1991)

As already stated, the dietary adopted here conforms to the criteria of nutritional adequacy and is based on physical efficiency only, with a modest contribution for palatability and social norms. It should be stressed however that due to the fact that many children from low income families are in receipt of free school meals, it is possible that the criteria of nutritional adequacy may not be met. This is as a result of the abolition of nutritional standards and price controls for school meals in the 1980 Education Act, which resulted in many local authorities increasing their prices which reduced the take-up rate of school meals. In addition the local authorities were prevented from providing free school meals for children from low income families, with the exceptions of those whose parents were in receipt of means-tested benefits. However the present nutritional content of the school meal has been found to be of a higher standard than meals purchased by children outside the school (CPAG). Although this is the case, it is not possible to predict with any degree of accuracy that the school meal complies with the nutritional standard used in this study; this would result in an under-estimation rather than an over-estimation of the nutritional adequacy of the children's diet. Whilst many children do receive school meals, there are many parents of children who have been excluded from these meals due to changes in the 1988 Social Security Act who now struggle to provide either the extra money for meals for their children or who are now forced to let their children purchase foods from local shops. Research has shown that the high fat and sugar content of many take-away foods are contributory factors in illness among the lower socio-economic classes. (Davey-Smith G. et al, 1990) The correlation between social class and morbidity is now irrefutable with research findings reporting a higher incidence of ischaemic heart disease among manual workers as opposed to non-manual workers. 'Poverty not only brings the risk of a shorter lifespan, but it also means that the lives of adults and children are more likely to be ground down by illness and disability' (Oppenheim C., CPAG 1993, p.85). The fear of illness is a very real one which affects households on low incomes, with research verifying the validity of these fears, in higher perinatal mortality rates, higher rates of heart disease, reports of stunted growth among children receiving free school meals, and higher incidence of dental caries. (Oppenheim 1993, Cole-Hamilton 1991, GHS 1990) 'The effect of low income renders it meaningless to consider diet a matter solely of choice' (Cole-Hamilton & Lang 1986). It is neither lack of knowledge nor lack of thrift that causes some of the inequalities in health, it is the lack of an adequate income which denies families the freedom to choose a healthier lifestyle.

3 Fuel

Calculating the fuel element of his primary poverty standard in 1899 was much simpler than the complex nutritional exercises Rowntree was forced to undertake. He calculated:

1 bag of coal (of 10 stone) in summer	} Average 1.5 bags @ 1s./3d.
2 bags of coal ,, in winter	} per bag, say 1s./10d.

He found that the amount of fuel used did not vary much with the size of family as there was usually a fire in the living room only. The price of coal during the winter of 1899 was about 1s./7d. per bag. Rowntree consulted a large coal merchant in York who informed him however that 1s./3d. was the average price. He commented that the working class, partly because they bought their coal by the bag, and partly because they purchased a wasteful coal which burned up quickly, paid as a rule, a price for their coal, higher by 25% than those who bought their coal by the ton). This time, Rowntree did not allow any extra for this 'the poor pay more' phenomenon.

In 1936, Rowntree simply based his estimates on the amounts spent each week on fuel (including lighting):

4s./4d. per week averaged over the whole year -
coal 2s./7d. per 10-stone bag (equal to 2/1 per cwt);

gas 7s./9d per therm and;
electricity 2.5d per unit.
(For details of the various items in Rowntree's fuel budget standard, see Appendix 6, p. 155 of his 1936 book.)

And in 1950, Rowntree and Laver interviewed approximately 30 households and obtained information about their expenditure on coal, coke, electricity and gas in the summer and winter months. This, averaged out over the entire sample of households with two adults and three children was 7s./7d. weekly for fuel and light.

Rowntree had used two methods with which to assess the subsistence fuel standards of the families he was researching. In 1899 he based his budget on his own informed yet subjective opinion. He assumed that a family (of whatever size) would only need one bag of coal weekly in summer and two bags weekly in winter. (p.109) He then calculated a weekly average based on these two figures. In his subsequent surveys he used expenditure data from low income families with which to calculate his fuel budget. The decision was taken by the research team to use both methods and evaluate the findings in an effort to adhere to Rowntree's aim of creating an irreducible standard. In order to define a fuel budget which would meet the above criteria, the team had to decide which standards to use. The temperature should be sufficient so as not to injure health, as the thrust of Rowntree's study was that the budget devised should provide for physical efficiency. Only basic appliances deemed as essential were used in the calculations. Insulation levels used were in keeping with normative standards in the UK in 1992; the fuel type used was to be the most efficient available to the population. In creating a model of this standard and then applying the government's own calculations to the cost of heating such a home, a fuel budget can be created which could not be construed as wasteful or extravagant.

The next stage was to determine a heating standard which could be regarded as adequate for physical efficiency and conducive to illness prevention. Differing expectations and preferences of warmth for a variety of ages and occupations had been previously researched. (Collins 1986, Boardman 1992) In defining an acceptable standard, other factors had also to be taken into account, such as: how many rooms need to be heated; do they all require the same temperature; how are the variables of clothing type and activity levels, all of which have an impact on the warmth of an individual, to be considered? Research involving the elderly found that as temperature decreased the risk of morbidity increased. Collins (1986) found that between the temperatures ranges of 18°C and 24°C, there was no risk to sedentary healthy people. As temperatures began to reduce, the risks to health increased. Below 16°C, the risk of respiratory disease increased, below 12°C, the sample displayed cardiovascular strain, with the risk of hypothermia at temperatures below 6°C. So clearly, the elderly need temperatures of between 18°C and 24°C to avoid ill health. Other research has displayed similar preferences for temperatures ranging from 19.4°C for housewives with young children, to 21°C for students, dependent children and others. The unemployed were estimated at requiring temperatures of 21.2°C compared with 20°C for the employed. (Boardman 1991, p. 108) When income constraints are removed, as in a study of the comfort zone for office workers, dissatisfaction occurred when the temperature fell below the comfort zone, defined as 20-23°C. As Boardman points out, this research was important as it was conducted in a natural environment without the concerns of fuel bills. High fuel bills or the threat of them can cause considerable stress for families on low income. A family interviewed for this survey never used the central heating as they believed that the bills could not be met from their weekly benefit.

Design standards for domestic heating have produced a variety of temperatures over the last thirty years which have complemented and reinforced the preferred comfort levels found in research. However they mostly ascribe to a temperature for daytime heating in occupied rooms and make assumptions on levels of activity in the home. Unheated, unoccupied rooms can cause damp, mould growth and condensation which can have deleterious consequences for health, both perceived and proven. (Davey-Smith et al., BMJ 1990) A mother sampled in this survey blamed the lack of heating in the bedrooms for her baby son's asthma; ideally she would like a mobile heater but could not afford the purchase or running costs. Research has shown that fear of high fuel bills is a very real one for families on low incomes. The Policy Studies Institute's (PSI) report 'Credit and Debt' (1992) found that, 'electricity and gas debts were more strongly associated with poverty than any other commitment: the mean income of those owing money was only £120 per week'. (p.150)

The various temperature requirements quoted point overwhelmingly to the need for whole house heating, an assumption which is supported by official data, with 80% of all households now having central heating systems. (Family Spending 1991) At the lower end of the income scale, there are approximately one out of every three households without central heating and many who have central heating but who do not use it due to the prospect of high bills (Cohen 1992). Again it is worth considering that the Family Spending survey does not collect data from those households residing in bed and breakfast accommodation or who live in institutions. (Johnson & Webb 1990) It is unclear how these omissions would impact on the results but the fact does remain that the lower down the income scale, the lower the access to central heating. Surprisingly it has never been a requirement of British standards that a domestic building should contain a heating system. (Boardman, p.223) Boardman points out that the British government may be if fact in breach of the universal declaration of human rights, which states that, 'Everyone has the right to a standard of living for the health and well-being of himself and his family'.

Good levels of insulation reduce fuel consumption and conserve heat produced; as much as 20% of an energy bill can be saved by having adequate loft insulation. (Boardman 1991) The cost of heating the typical semi-detached house in the UK, described by the Dept. of Energy's Energy Efficiency Office (EEO) as one which has 50mm. loft insulation, a 25mm. hot water cylinder insulation jacket, 25% double glazing and room thermostats, is, on average, £445 per annum. This cost for whole house space and water heating achieves a temperature for morning and evening (approximately eleven hours) of 21°C in living room and does not include standing charges. The reality is such that, according to Brescu, nearly 90% of the housing stock was built before the 1976 thermal insulation standards came into effect, with a vast proportion still inadequately insulated. The picture emerges of housing stock which has loft insulation and hot water cylinder jacket - but little else.

Boardman deduced that temperatures of 21°C in occupied rooms during daytime hours would be required for health and comfort with increases slightly above for vulnerable groups. In unoccupied rooms, a temperature of 14°C is advised with which to prevent condensation. Bedrooms should be no less than 16°C at night for vulnerable groups in order to prevent respiratory diseases. It is also known that during the winter months there are 8,000 excess deaths for each C° reduction, and with UK homes considerably colder than other European countries, they therefore need more expenditure in order to purchase more warmth. This is bound to be an issue of concern not only in terms of the health of all low income groups but also the number of excess deaths which may be caused by fuel poverty.

In view of the authoritative results of research already completed in the field of energy requirements and using the Energy Efficiency Office's (EEO) own recommendations, it was decided that central heating running costs should also form part of the fuel budget on the grounds that the lack of it would impair physical efficiency. Initially the team opted for the collection of actual fuel expenditure data for two reasons: firstly, that it would give a true reflection of expenditure patterns among low income households and; secondly the findings could be compared with the expenditure data of similar income groups and family types. The data was collected during interviews in which the researcher requested (where available) the previous year's fuel bills. Only three of the respondents were able to comply. However the remainder of the sample had prior arrangements with the energy companies which resulted in them being able to give a weekly, fortnightly or monthly payment figure which was constant for the year. Where respondents had fuel bill arrears within the estimate, these were deducted by the researcher to give the current weekly fuel budget. The findings bore out what the team had expected - fuel expenditure was higher than that found in the official statistics. The following table illustrates the variance found amongst the sample:

Table 3.1
Weekly fuel expenditure of 1992 sample

Gas	Electricity	Total
4.00	8.00	12.00
6.00	12.50	18.50
8.15	10.00	18.15
---	10.00	10.00
11.00	13.00	24.00
2.12	20.00	22.12
4.50	10.00	14.50
5.50	15.00	20.50
6.25	9.00	15.25
4.75	10.00	14.75
5.00	10.00	15.00
11.25	13.75	25.00
9.80	11.50	21.30
8.49	8.00	16.49
4.16	10.39	14.55
15.00	16.00	31.00
7.50	10.00	17.50
8.00	11.00	19.00

The average obtained from this sample amounted to £18.31 weekly. This compares very unfavourably with the average weekly household fuel expenditure contained in the Family Spending report for our moderate family type and among all households receiving incomes similar to the families interviewed. The data collected from this sample did not take into account all the variables which impacted on the fuel expenditure of the sample. These variables included the number of appliances and the extent of their usage, the type of heating, fuel and length of time in use, as well as insulation levels, housing size, type and structure. It was felt that fuel expenditure could not be used as an tool for defining needs in the same way that food expenditure could not possibly define the amount needed for an adequate / subsistence diet. The dissimilarity between official fuel expenditure data and the findings from this study perhaps illustrate the difficulties of using expenditure data as opposed to objective scientific methods, those preferred by Rowntree in 1899. The results vindicated the decision to explore Rowntree's alternative method of establishing a fuel budget standard which he had based on his own informed assumptions. The following table shows the differences between the various estimations, either actual fuel expenditure or fuel budget standards:

Table 3.2
Comparison of actual fuel expenditure data and official statistics

(Family Spending 92)	Weekly Income	Average Fuel Expenditure / Needs	Percentage 1991 Income
All Households	£100-£125	£10.55	8.4%-10.5%
One man,one woman and two children	£275 (and under)	£13.56	5%
'Rowntree 1992' Fuel budget	£105	£18.31	17%

By using the government's own statistics and the work of experts in the field of fuel poverty and budget standards, it was possible to arrive at a subsistence fuel budget standard for a family of four on low income. The team acknowledged that one weekly figure for fuel expenditure could not validly be submitted as representative without supporting evidence which ideally should include insulation levels, housing type and fuel type and efficiency. In the absence of such data from this study, it was decided that a minimum fuel budget could be determined for a variety of housing types by using updated figures previously published by the Energy Efficiency Office (1986), and applying them to distinct housing types with differing insulation levels. (Stitt 1991) Using data on housing type and socio-economic grouping from the General Household Survey and the EEO's updated Monergy figures, it was possible to establish a general housing type which could be used as a model for a minimum fuel budget. (EEO 1986)

Using the data within the General Household Survey, it was possible to determine that, amongst households with weekly incomes of £150 or less, terraced housing is more common than any other housing type. According to the Family Spending report, 65%-70% of low income households now have either full or partial central heating, compared with an average of 80% for all income groups and 88% of all families comprising two adults and two children: 'Central heating has come to be perceived as a necessity rather than a luxury....market penetration of central heating is spreading down the income scale, with the most popular form of central heating being gas fired.' (Mintel 1989) Strong correlations have been found between poor loft insulation and the lower socio-economic groups, with households in the lower income groups generally having poorer levels of insulation in their homes. (Boardman 1991) There are many types of insulation methods which include double glazing, cavity wall insulation, pipe lagging, draughtproofing and use of boiler jackets. Many of the newer homes now have fitted as standard a certain level of insulation, such as loft insulation and cylinder jackets. The next table shows that the levels of insulation of low income households are far from ideal and this alone will have the effect of increasing fuel expenditure for low income households:

Table 3.3

Percentage of households with insulation by socio-economic group

	Loft	Full Cavity Wall/Ins	Cavity+ Loft Ins + D/Glazing
AB	87	23	17
C1	80	18	10
C2	77	15	6
D	69	9	1
E	68	9	1

(Cited in Boardman 1991)

It is partly because lower income groups live in poorly insulated housing that they are having to spend more in order to heat their homes. In addition to this, they are not able to shop around for a cheaper fuel as they could with food or clothing. The newer homes with the better insulation standards are in the main occupied by better off families, and generally they have access to more efficient gas heating systems. So the situation is this, that poorer people with less money have to spend more of their already stretched incomes in order to heat their inefficiently insulated homes with inefficient heating systems. This is the general model which would apply to low income groups, but for the sake of creating a minimum fuel budget standard, this normative model will not be used without very important qualifications and alterations.

So it has been established that the most economical fuel available is gas, coupled with increased access to central heating down the socio-economic strata. This information is then combined with the findings of the GHS to establish a typical housing type for low income households and reveals the typical home of a low income household as being mainly terraced housing, with relatively poor insulation levels. To use the low insulated model on which to base the minimum fuel budget would leave the study open the criticism that we used the circumstances which would most enhance and increase the cost of home heating, although the existing data does show that these circumstances do prevail among low income households. For these reasons, our estimates for fuel are serious under-estimations for the majority of poor families. For the purposes of establishing a minimum fuel budget; the figures quoted will include both loft insulation and cylinder jacket insulation of the type which is most prevalent in the UK as a whole today, as specified by the Energy Efficiency Office (EEO 1992). If this model is then combined with the heating requirements necessary to provide for physical efficiency, for a household living on Income Support (as the definitive indicator of a poor household), thus incurring the extra expense due to longer hours spent in the home, it is then possible, using the EEOs own figures, uprated to 1992 prices to calculate a minimum needs fuel budget for a variety of housing types. The model is not representative of all household types or dwelling but it is comparable to the type most prevalent for this income group. Table 3.4 illustrates how the composition of the final fuel budget standard was compiled:

Table 3.4
Estimated weekly fuel costs for gas heated terraced house.

	Nov 1985	uprated to 1992
Space Heating	6.92	8.82
Hot water	1.21	1.54
Cooking	.58	.74
Electrical Appliances	2.14	2.73
+ Standing Charge		1.60
Total		15.43

Sources: Monergy (Gas) Energy Efficiency Office (1986)
Stitt S (1991)

In putting this figure of £15.43 forward as a minimum fuel budget, the team are mindful of the actual expenditure data collected from the sample as being almost £3 more than the sum specified. In using the lower figure on which to base the fuel budget, the research team feel they are justified in describing it as an irreducible fuel budget.

In March 1993, the Chancellor of the Exchequer announced that domestic fuel purchases would, in future, be subject to VAT. Amid an outcry from politicians and fuel poverty groups that this would represent a further tax on the poor, the Chancellor suggested that some welfare might be compensated for this increase in the price of warmth. At the time of writing, it is clear that most poor households will simply face a VAT-rated increase on the costs of keeping their homes warm and dry and that a primary poverty line in Britain in 1993 must take account of this. For example, our 1992 subsistence fuel budget standard would cost in 1994, £18.13 plus inflation.

Table 3.6

Summary of weekly flea counts for gas control treated houses.

4 Clothing and footwear

In his first work in 1899, Rowntree included, under the heading of 'household sundries', all necessary expenditure other than food and house rent, the principal items being 'boots, clothes and fuel'. He did not say how many respondents he interviewed nor how many estimates he averaged. His estimates for minimum expenditure necessary for household sundries was based upon information gathered from an unspecified number of working people. 'Many of those interviewed knew what poverty meant and had learned from hard experience what could be "done without", and how to obtain most cheaply, that which was absolutely necessary.' Dealing with men's clothes, the information which was asked from the men was briefly this: 'What, in your opinion, is the lowest sum upon which a man can keep himself in clothing for a year? The clothing should be adequate to keep the man in health and should not be so shabby as to injure his chances of obtaining respectable employment. Apart from these two considerations, the clothing to be the most economical obtainable.' Then his researchers went over every article of clothing, item by item, asking for information as to the cheapest ways in which these could be secured, and the average length of time these would last. In this way, he obtained a number of estimates of necessary expenditure for clothing upon which his final estimate was based. The estimates of necessary expenditure for women's and children's clothing, and for other household sundries such as fuel, light, soap, replacements etc. were similarly obtained by a female research from the women interviewed. Table 4.1 shows the average of the estimates he obtained. He found that the bulk of the estimates only varied within narrow limits. A few which were obviously too high were not used in his calculations. These figures were adopted for the purposes of his 1899 inquiry as representing the minimum necessary expenditure for household sundries:

Table 4.1
Clothing estimates obtained by Rowntree in 1899

	Per Year	Per Week
Man	26/-	6d
Woman	26/-	6d
Boy of 12	27/-)Average	Average (6d)
Child of 2	17/-) 22/-*	5d (4d

(*This average price has been taken to be the minimum necessary expenditure for clothes for all children under 16 years of age.) (pp. 107/8)

In introducing this area of need in his 'Human Needs of Labour' calculations in 1936, Rowntree explained that his purpose was to arrive at the minimum sum which a working class family must spend on such clothing as was necessary 'to keep the body warm and dry and to maintain a modest respectability'. In order to 'obtain reliable information', he made inquiries among a number of men and women 'who knew from first-hand information as to how low a cost it was possible to clothe a family'. (p. 94) His data collection led him to conclude that, regarding men's clothing, if he excluded certain estimates which were higher than the rest, of the twelve remaining replies, the estimates varied from 2s./6d. to 3s./6d. and so he adopted a figure of 3 shillings. Regarding women's clothing, twelve estimates varied from 1s./6d. to 2s./4d. and so, he took 1s./9d. as his figure. He then obtained forty estimates of the costs of the necessary clothing for children of different ages, which naturally varied according to age, but they indicated generally an all round estimate of 1s./1d. per week for children. This aggregated at eight shillings a week for a family of five. (The detailed information on which these estimates were based is given in Appendix F, pp. 153/4 of Rowntree's 1936 book). (pp. 94/5)

Again, in applying optimum stringency, tinged with moral acceptability and practical reality, he added: 'I have made no allowance for any gifts of old clothing which may be received. In fixing minimum wages, we have no right to assume charitable gifts which are, at best, exceedingly precarious; and moreover, it is becoming increasingly useful for well-to-do families to dispose of their old clothes to second-hand dealers, instead of giving them away.' (pp. 95/6) Based on this, second-hand clothing was not a realistic option for the purposes of this study, although hand-down clothing and footwear influenced the costings. Referring to what he perceived as the idiosyncratic nature of women's clothing needs, he explained: 'In the case of women workers, the great majority of whom are unmarried, an allowance at a considerably higher rate must be made. A girl who cannot afford to dress nicely will be seriously handicapped in the matter of marriage. Quite apart from vanity, she rightly and naturally desires to look her best. The allowance for clothing and shoes for a woman worker who has to keep herself cannot be put at less than 5s./3d. a week.' (p. 108)

Clothing for men included estimates for: suits, overcoat, mackintosh, coat and flannel trousers, footwear, shirts (day and night), vest and pants, socks, overalls, hats and caps, sundries. (p.153) Clothing for married women and women workers included estimates for: costume, winter coat, summer coat, mackintosh, dresses, skirts, blouses, jumpers, underclothing, stockings, hats, overalls, sundries (gloves, mufflers, handkerchiefs). (p. 154)

To ascertain the clothing requirements of women and children in 1950, Rowntree and Laver explained that one of their female researchers interviewed 29 women in order to ascertain how much they spent on clothing for themselves and their children and on household sundries. All of them were women whose husbands earned less than £6 a week. They found that varying 'degrees of economy' were practised and the average expenditure on women's clothing and repairs was 11s./4d. a week, which included 51s./2d. for boot repairs, and on children's clothing and repairs was 9s./6d. per week. In view of the great variation in the expenditure on women's, children's and men's clothing, they concluded that it would have been misleading to have based their poverty line on the **average** expenditure incurred by all the families who supplied them with information. As they were cautious to establish a poverty line which no one could reasonably claim was too high, they based it on the average expenditure of three women whose actual spending on clothing was the lowest and they exercised the same approach in the case of expenditure on children's clothing and household sundries. The figures arrived at were 5s./2d. a week for women's clothing, 5s./6d. a week for children's clothing and 6 shillings for household sundries. (pp. 14/5) Rowntree & Laver gave no explanation as to why they changed the approach in estimating minimum clothing and household needs from seeking the opinions of poor households themselves, as in 1899 and 1936, to citing actual expenditure - especially among the very poorest/lowest spending whose expenditure patterns are influenced most be income constraints and to a much less degree, by needs, albeit of a subsistence nature.

On necessary expenditure on men's clothing, interviews similar to those held with 29 women were held with 32 men and their annual expenditure on clothing and repairs was established. This showed that the average expenditure of all the men was 9s./11d. on clothing and repairs, but, as in the case of women, for the purpose of building up their poverty line, they considered only the average expenditure of the three men whose expenditure was the lowest. This was 6s./1d. a week for clothing. (pp. 15/16) Adding amounts for the repairs of footwear, they found that none of their estimates included the cost of repairs. Taking the 29 families whose expenditure was investigated in 1950, the cost of repairing children's boots and shoes averaged 9d. per child per week. (p. 16)

Returning to the perceived improvement in the standards of living of the poor and the impact of this on Rowntree's own research, they added that, in 1950, the variations in expenditure were very much greater than in 1936. In the case of women's clothing, they varied from 4s./4d. a week to 19s./6d., in children's clothing from 5s./3d. to 20s./9d. and in men's clothing from 5s./5d. to 16s./11d. a week. They suspected that the reasons why the variations in the expenditure per head were so much greater in 1950 than in 1936 was, 'doubtless because working class families are enjoying increased prosperity and so there is a marginal sum of money available after paying for the bare necessities of life, which can be spent according to personal inclination'. (pp. 16/17)

In determining a minimum clothing budget for his study, Rowntree had decided to use the opinions of his sample with which to inform the study. He believed that they were the 'real experts' and they alone knew how best to budget for clothing far more wisely than academic or professional 'experts' would; they too would know the most economical prices available with which to cost the clothing and footwear. He was mindful to stress that the clothing should not be so shabby as to injure a person's chances of obtaining employment; he was also at pains to stress the need for a little extra for young women in order that they might look their best so as not to spoil their chances of attracting the attentions of the opposite sex. The question posed in 1899 to the families of York was put verbatim to the families in the 1992 study. It is worth repeating: 'What, in your opinion is the very lowest sum upon which a man (family) can keep himself (themselves) in clothing for a year? The clothing should be adequate to keep the man (family) in health and should not be so shabby as to injure his (their) chances of obtaining respectable employment.'

The clothing estimates Rowntree gained from his families were to be at the lowest obtainable costs. The 1992 study followed Rowntree's format as closely as possible. With the aid of clothing lists, the researcher went through each item of clothing on the list and asked how many were needed, how long they would last and at what price they could be purchased using the most economical means available to the families. From the eighteen families interviewed, valid estimates were obtained for fifteen women, twelve men and twenty-eight children. Some estimates received were deemed too high and in keeping with Rowntree's methods, these estimates were not included. Based on the estimates obtained, the cost of keeping a family in clothing for one year using the most reasonable costings available would amount to £1,352. The following table illustrates how the weekly costs vary between family members:

Table 4.2
Clothing estimates obtained in 1992

Man	Woman	Child 7-11yrs	Child 4-6yrs	Total
£6.49	£5.92	£7.42	£6.17	£26.00

Families who receive Income Support are eligible to apply for Clothing Grants from their local authority, as are other low income families; these grants are means tested and are administered on a sliding scale. They are however discretionary, and at the time of publishing, some authorities have reported serious financial difficulties managing their education budgets. One way they have practised to limit expenditure has been to reduce or abolish the clothing grants payable to families. These grants are a welcome help towards the cost of providing uniforms for the children, and curtailing assistance to these vulnerable groups will only serve to push the families concerned further into debt in order obtain school uniforms. In order to reflect the financial assistance this grant makes (in theory) to the clothing budget, the grant was divided by 52 to obtain the weekly cost and this was deducted from the estimates, giving the weekly total for the family of £24.34. It must be stated that it is the view of the research team that this amount is not sufficient to purchase for all the families' clothing and footwear needs. Often such sums are used to buy the largest item such as the winter coat, with the other smaller less expensive garments purchased from the remaining weekly budget.

The National Foster Care Association have devised scales which are used to assess the financial needs of children. Foster carers have informed the Association that it can take as much as 50% more to look after a child in foster care than to look after a family's own children. If the minimum allowance is broken down as suggested by the NFCA into its component parts, we can compare actual expenditure with the clothing allowances of those children in foster care. The NFCA estimate that 18% of the minimum weekly allowance should be spent on clothing. The following table shows the allowances and estimated costs of clothing for foster children:

Table 4.3
Estimated costs of clothing for foster children

Age	(a) Minimum Allowance	(b) Clothing 18% of (a)	(c) 1992 (this study) Estimate
5-7	£57.82	£10.40	£6.17 (4-6 yrs)
8-10	£63.28	£11.39	£7.42 (7-11 yrs)
11-12	£68.81	£12.38	

Source: National Foster Care Association (1993)

The importance of using the experience of families with which to assess clothing needs as opposed to expert opinion is illustrated by some of the unrealistic lifespans given by experts to some items of children's clothing, e.g., winter socks having a lifespan of two years. If a child's feet grow so rapidly as to need shoes replacing every three months, it would seem absurd to suggest that they have the same pair of socks for two years, unless of course they are passed on to another child. Similarly the rate of growth of the child can limit the lifespan available; a pair of school trousers may still be in good condition after two years, but it is debatable whether the child would wear them or fit into them, given the growth rate which occurs in a two year period. How long an item of clothing or footwear lasts is dependent on a number of factors as has already been stated. Quality of the clothing is an important factor. Many of the items costed in this study were relatively inexpensive items but their lifespans were correspondingly less than expected due to the inferior quality of the garments and individual wear and tear. One mother knew from experience how unpredictable it can be to assign a lifespan to children's clothing. Her eight year old son, only two days into the new school term, had returned home with holes in the knees of his new school trousers. They were irreparable and, as she did not have the money to spare from the family budget to replace them immediately, she was forced to keep the child away from school. The child only possessed one pair of jeans and she would not send him to school in them for fear of him being sent home, as had happened in the past. She had to borrow the money from relatives to eventually replace the item.

Durability of children's footwear seemed to be a major cause of concern for parents due to a number of reasons. Firstly, replacement costs were felt to be extremely high, with quality shoes in some instances costing as much as adult shoes despite the absence of VAT (presently) on children's items. The rate of growth varies between children with some parents unable to keep up with the expense incurred. Some children needed shoes replacing as often as every six weeks during rapid growth or due to excessive wear and tear. If one looks at the list of standard items used by the old Supplementary Benefit Commission, allowance can only be made for one pair of shoes and the only other footwear specified is a pair of slippers. (Stitt 1989) If a claimant presented himself every six weeks for a special payment for children's shoes, his/her chances of receiving help would have been very slim.

Peer pressure from other children was also a problem which parents had to deal with. Parents were able to determine the type of shoe the child wore but only up to a certain age. Training shoes are one such item, as the child becomes more socially aware, it can be a very difficult for parents to accommodate the socially perceived needs of their offspring (Ward et al 1977), who are subject to the intense pressure exerted by the advertising industry, especially in the case of training shoes or sports wear of any kind. It would be futile and expensive for parents to impose their own choices upon their children as invariably the shoes or garments would not be worn, a point made by a mother who had bought a pair of 'unnamed' training shoes for her twelve year old son from a local market. He refused to wear them preferring to wear his worn out but 'named' trainers instead. Many of these expensive purchases can be made through using mail-order catalogues with the cost spread out over a longer period helping to spread the weekly cost. Berthoud and Kempson (1992) found that, 'credit commitments represent only a small proportion of the available income of rich families, but proportion rises with lower incomes ... at the extreme the (expenditure) exceeded the available income. The whole of their budgets has now been accounted for with no leeway at all.' (p.104)

It is not unusual therefore for families on low incomes to place clothing at the bottom of their list of essentials. One family had only £20 left out of their weekly income with which to purchase food, after all other commitments were met, but these commitments did not include clothing; they simply could not budget for clothes and relied solely on their parents to purchase clothing for them at birthdays and Xmas. An example of the how one woman budgeted for clothing for her children illustrated just how little was available within the income of this family to provide for clothing. The woman gave £1 each week to her mother to save for her, her mother also put £1 in the weekly 'fund' and this enabled small purchases of clothing to be made occasionally without severely curtailing expenditure on other essentials such as food.

Avoiding false economy was the reason given by a male respondent for purchasing expensive boots rather than a cheaper version. He had purchased a pair of boots for £75 from a mail order catalogue, not by choice, he added; if he had the cash, he would have bought the same boots from a shop for less cost. The rationale for this expensive purchase was that he would expect them to last for at least five years and they would be versatile in that he could use them for walking, of which he did a lot due to his lack of income and the relatively high cost of local transport; he also expected them to double as workboots should he obtain work. He had one pair of shoes which he paid 'a lot for', they have lasted six years, and are saved for interviews; the only other footwear is a pair of slippers which he regularly obtains as Xmas presents. He was correct in his assertion that it would have been false economy to buy the cheaper shoes as this was tested by the researcher when comparing other lifespans and estimates for cheaper shoes. The problem for many families is that they do not have access to this kind of money nor is there any leeway in the budget to allow for purchases of this nature to be made via catalogues. Although a lifeline to many, catalogue payments can suck the family deeper into debt. (Cohen et al, CPAG 1992) This man's estimates were particularly low at just £2.66 weekly, compared to the average adult male estimates of £6.49.

High estimates were received from one family who had only recently made the transition from a two-adult earner family, to one which was now reliant on Income Support (due to redundancy). The mother remarked that the money she was now receiving on Income Support was almost as much as she used to spend on her food bill each week, when working. This lady only knew the costings for clothing from Marks and Spencers and she firmly believed that they were the best value for money giving longer lifespan and better quality. When this family's clothing list was constructed, it was found that the estimates were indeed too high to be included in the calculations for a minimum clothing budget. It was obvious from this lady's estimates that she had yet to begin budgeting for clothing out of the Income Support allowance. Indeed her own personal estimation of a minimum clothing budget for herself amounted to £9.12 weekly which is approximately 8% of the total weekly income of the whole household; this is extremely high if one compares the percentage expenditure of clothing for the whole family in relation to the income of the household in the Family Spending report, where clothing amounts to 7% of the total expenditure. This raises and answers the question about the accessibility of good quality clothing in terms of the pricing of high street clothing retailers and who exactly they are aiming their produce at.

The low income families in the survey invariably cited the costings of clothing from their most recent experience, either at local markets or in the low cost clothing outlets. Ethel Austin's pricing was quoted widely as representing reasonable quality clothing at economical prices. Obviously each area will have their own particular clothing stores from which economic costings can be obtained. There will also be many areas which are not served by such outlets and in using the estimates of families who do have access to such competitive pricing and thus the study once again errs on the side of underestimation of the clothing costs of families.

The following pages include the clothing lists used as guidelines and pointers by the study to determine the clothing budget. Rowntree's question was asked verbatim: 'What in your opinion is the very lowest sum which a man (family) can keep himself (itself) in clothing per year? The clothing should be adequate to keep him (them) in health. It should not be so shabby as to injure his (their) chances of obtaining respectable employment. It should be the most economical obtainable.' The following lists were used to guide the families. Columns two to four show the ranges of quantities, costs and lifespans given to the researcher, the last column contains average weekly cost per item after cost, quantity, and lifespan were taken into account for each person in the household:

MAN'S CLOTHING

	NUMBER OF ITEMS	COST PER ITEM £	EXPECTED LIFE YEARS	WEEKLY COST £
SUIT	1	35 - 70	2 - 5	0.304
JEANS	1 - 3	10 - 30	.5 - 3	0.798
TROUSER	1 - 3	10 - 20	2 - 5	0.352
WINTER COAT	0 - 1	25 - 50	1 - 3	0.479
ANORAK	1	20 - 30	1 - 5	0.182
SHIRTS	2 - 5	5 - 15	1 - 3	0.291
BEST SHIRT	1	6 - 20	3 - 5	0.127
TIE	1	3 - 5	5 - 10	0.071
T-SHIRTS	3 - 6	3 - 5	1 - 3	0.232
WINTER JUMPER	1 - 3	5 - 15	2 - 5	0.340

SWEAT SHIRT	1 - 3	5 - 15	2 - 5	0.266
SHORTS	1 - 2	5 - 10	2 - 5	0.115
SWIM TRUNKS	1	5 - 10	2 - 5	0.034
UNDER -PANTS	4 - 8	1 - 3	1 - 2	0.228
PYJAMAS	0 - 1	5 - 10	3 - 5	0.035
DRESSING GOWN	1	7 - 15	3 - 7	0.057
SOCKS	5 - 8	1 - 2.50	1 - 2	0.232
SCARF	1	2 - 3	5+	0.017
GLOVES	1 - 2	2 - 5	2 - 5	0.023
WINTER HAT	1	2 - 3	3 - 6	0.043
BELT	1 - 2	2 - 7	3 - 10	0.049
SMART SHOES	1	12 - 30	2 - 5	0.247
WALKING SHOES	1	10 - 25	1 - 5	0.158
TRAINERS	1 - 3	10 - 30	1 - 3	0.452
SLIPPERS	1	3 - 5	1 - 3	0.092
TRACK SUIT	2 - 5	20 - 35	2 - 5	0.23
KAGOUL	2 - 10	5 - 10	3 - 7	0.30
JACKET	2 - 7	20 - 35	3 - 7	0.226
BOOTS	2 - 5	25 - 75	2 - 5	0.064
GILET	2 - 10	5 - 10	3 - 8	0.092

WOMAN'S CLOTHING

ITEM	NUMBER OF ITEMS	COST PER ITEM £	EXPECTED LIFE YEARS	WEEKLY COST £
ANORAK	1	15 - 50	1 - 4	0.128
SUMMER SKIRT	1 - 3	1 - 3	1 - 3	0.144
WINTER SKIRT	1 - 3	1 - 3	1 - 3	0.153
JEANS	2 - 4	2 - 4	2 - 4	0.570
SHORTS	1 - 3	1 - 3	0 - 4	0.067
TROUS-ERS	0 - 1	4	1	0.153
SWEAT SHIRT	2 - 3	2 - 3	1 - 3	0.144
WINTER JUMPER	2 - 3	2 - 3	2 - 3	0.280
CARDI-GAN	0 - 5	0 - 5	0 - 3	0.153
SMART BLOUSE	1	5 - 10	2 - 5	0.096
BLOUSE	2	0 - 4	0 - 6	0.280
T-SHIRT	4 - 5	3 - 7	2 - 3	0.340
SWIMSUIT	1	5 - 7	1 - 5	0.076
NIGHT-DRESS	2 - 3	3 - 5	2 - 4	0.173
DRESSING GOWN	1 - 2	6 - 10	3 - 5	0.185
BRIEFS	5 - 10	.80 - 1	1 - 3	0.460
BRAS	3 - 5	3 - 4	.5 - 3	0.650

WAIST SLIPS	**0 - 3**	**0 - 2**	**0 - 3**	**0.057**
TIGHTS	**3 - 10**	**1**	**1 - 2 wks**	**0.500**
WINTER TIGHTS	**1 - 3**	**3**	**0 - 1**	**0.096**
SOCKS	**4 - 5**	**1**	**1 - 2**	**0.115**
WINTER HAT	**0**	**0**	**0**	
SCARF	**1**	**3**	**2 - 5**	**0.028**
GLOVES	**1**	**2 - 3**	**2 - 5**	**0.028**
SMART SHOES	**1**	**15 - 20**	**1 - 2**	**0.1-5**
EVERY DAY SHOES	**2 - 3**	**6 - 10**	**1 - 3**	**0.058**
TRAINERS	**1 - 2**	**6 - 20**	**1 - 4**	**0.380**
SANDALS	**1**	**5 - 10**	**1 - 4**	**0.046**
WINTER COAT	**0 - 1**	**0 - 50**	**2 - 7**	**0.320**
TRACK-SUIT	**0 - 1**	**0 - 20**	**2 - 3**	**0.570**
BOOTS	**0 - 1**	**0 - 20**	**2 - 5**	**0.280**
SLIPPERS	**1 - 2**	**4 - 6**	**1 - 2**	**0.038**

GIRL 4 - 6 YEARS CLOTHING ESTIMATES

ITEM	NUMBER OF ITEMS	COST PER ITEM	EXPECTED LIFE YEARS	WEEKLY COST
WINTER COAT	1 - 2	20 - 30	1 - 2	0.760
SUMMER COAT	1 - 2	5 - 10	1 - 2	0.480
BEST DRESS	1 - 2	10	1	0.480
WINTER DRESS	0 - 2	0 - 8	1	0.570
SUMMER DRESS	2 - 3	0 - 5	1 - 2	1.150
TRACK-SUIT	2 - 3	8 - 10	1 - 3	1.150
DUNGAR-EES	1 - 2	6 - 7	1 - 2	0.580
CARDI-GANS	2 - 3	4 - 6	1	1.150
JUMPERS	2 - 4	4 - 5	1 - 2	0.920
TROUSER	1 - 3	0 - 2	1 - 2	0.460
SHOES	2 - 3	8 - 13	.3 - 1	0.860
TRAINERS	0 - 2	0 - 10	1	0.760
SLIPPERS	1 - 2	3	1	0.096
SANDALS	0 - 1	0 - 5	1	0.380
PUMPS	0 - 1	0 - 2	1	0.380
WELLING-TONS	1	6 - 8	1	0.144
SWIMSUIT	1	4 - 5	1 - 3	0.192

BRIEFS	7 - 10	.35 - 1.20	.5 - 1	0.760
VESTS	4 - 8	1 - 1.50	.5 - 1	0.096
PETTI-COATS	0 - 2	3 - 6	1 - 2	0.115
PYJAMAS	2 - 4	3 - 5	1 - 2	0.280
DRESSING GOWN	1 - 2	5 - 6	1 - 3	0.192
SLEEP-SUIT	0 - 2	4 - 8	0 - 2	0.064
LONG SOCKS	2 - 7	1 - 1.50	.5 - 1	0.280
ANKLE SOCKS	2 - 6	.80 - 1.50	.5 - 1	0.192
WINTER TIGHTS	2 - 4	2	.5 - 1	0.230
SHORTS	2 - 4	3	1 - 2	0.460
T-SHIRTS	3 - 6	3	1	0.570
WINTER HAT	0 - 2	3	2 - 4	0.010
SCARF	1	2 - 3	2 - 4	0.019
GLOVES/ MITTENS	1	1 - 2	1 - 2	0.038

GIRL'S 7 - 11

WINTER COAT	**1 - 2**	**20 -25**	**2**	**0.480**
SUMMER COAT	**1 - 2**	**10- 15**	**2**	**0.286**
BEST DRESS	**1**	**10 - 15**	**1**	**0.428**
WINTER DRESS	**1**	**10**	**1**	**0.380**
SUMMER DRESS	**2**	**8 - 10**	**1**	**0.308**
SUIT	**1 - 2**	**8 - 15**	**1**	**0.394**
DUNGAR-EES	**2**	**8 - 15**	**1 - 2**	**0.360**
CARDI-GANS	**2**	**5 - 8**	**1 - 2**	**0.236**
JUMPERS	**2 - 4**	**7 - 10**	**1 - 2**	**0.350**
TROUSER	**2**	**4 - 10**	**1 - 2**	**0.142**
SHOES	**1 - 2**	**10 - 15**	**.5 - 1**	**0.286**
TRAINERS	**1 - 2**	**10 - 15**	**.5 - 1**	**0.425**
SLIPPERS	**1**	**2 - 4**	**.5 - 1**	**0.280**
SANDALS	**1**	**7 - 10**	**.5 - 1**	**0.280**
PUMPS	**1**	**2 - 2.50**	**.5 - 1**	**0.058**
WELLING TONS	**1**	**6.50 - 8**	**1**	**0.420**
SWIMSUIT	**1**	**5 - 7**	**1 - 2**	**0.278**
PANTS	**5 - 7**	**.80 - 1**	**.5**	**0.226**
VESTS	**4 - 5**	**1 - 1.5**	**.5 - 1**	**0.153**

PETTI-COATS	**0 - 1**	**2**	**1 - 2**	**0.280**
PYJAMAS	**2 - 3**	**5 - 6**	**.5 - 3**	**0.570**
DRESSING GOWN	**1**	**8 - 10**	**1 - 3**	**0.533**
SLEEP-SUIT	**0**			
LONG SOCKS	**4 - 5**	**.75 - 1.50**	**.5 - 1**	**0.050**
ANKLE SOCKS	**5 - 7**	**.75 - 1**	**.25 - 1**	**0.580**
WINTER TIGHTS	**2 - 3**	**2.50 - 5**	**.25 - 1**	**0.480**
SHORTS	**3 - 4**	**3 - 5**	**.5 - 2**	**0.038**
T-SHIRTS	**4 - 6**	**2 - 5**	**.5 - 1**	**0.380**
WINTER HAT	**1**	**2 - 4**	**1 - 2**	**0.153**
SCARF	**1**	**2 - 3**	**2 - 4**	**0.380**
GLOVES/ MITTENS	**1 - 2**	**2 - 4**	**1 - 2**	**0.323**

BOY 4 - 6 YEARS CLOTHING ESTIMATE

ITEM	NUMBER OFD	COST £	EXPECTED LIFE YEARS	WEEKLY COST £
WINTER COAT	1	10 - 25	1 - 2	0.038
SUMMER JACKET	1	10	1 - 2	0.222
TRACK-SUIT	1 - 3	10 - 15	1 - 2	0.422
JEANS	2	5 - 10	1 - 2	0.279
SHORTS	5	3 - 6	1	0.193
T-SHIRTS	5	3 - 5	1	0.238
BEST TROUSER	1	5 - 10	1	0.183
BEST SHIRT	1	5 - 8	1	0.152
BEST JUMPER	1	5 - 10	1	0.230
SWEAT-SHIRT	5	5 - 8	1 - 1.5	0.282
SWIMSUIT	1	3 - 5	1 - 2	0.089
BOXERS/ BRIEF	5 - 7	1 - 1.50	.5 - 1	0.214
VESTS	4 - 7	1 - 1.75	1	0.155
PYJAMAS	0 - 2	5 - 7	1 - 2	0.202
DRESSING GOWN	0 - 1	10 - 15	1 - 2	0.062
WINTER SOCKS	3 - 5	1 - 1.5	1	0.115

SUMMER SOCKS	5 - 7	1 - 1.50	1	0.096
WINTER JUMPERS	2 - 4	5 - 7	1 - 2	0.208
WINTER HAT	0 - 1	2 - 3	2 - 4	0.136
SCARF	0 - 1	2 - 3	2 - 4	0.067
GLOVES	1 - 2	2 - 3	2 - 3	0.155
SHOES	2 - 3	10 - 15	.4 - 1	0.308
TRAINERS	1 - 2	10 - 20	.5 - 1	0.430
CANVAS PUMPS	1	2.50	1	0.059
WELLING TONS	1	7 - 8	1 - 2	0.110
SLIPPERS	1 - 2	3 - 5	1	0.072
SHIRT (SCHOOL)	2 - 4	5 - 7	1	0.180
TROUSER	2	5 - 7	1	0.246
PULL-OVER	2 - 3	5 - 9	1 - 2	0.152
KAGOUL	1	4 - 8	1 - 2	0.052
TIE	1	2 - 5	1 - 4	0.013
SHORTS	0 - 2	2 - 7	1	0.059
T-SHIRT	1 - 3	3 - 6	1 - 2	0.059
GYM-SHOES	1	3 - 5	1 - 2	0.059

BOY 7 - 11 YEARS CLOTHING ESTIMATES

ITEM	NUMBER OF ITEMS	COST PER ITEM £	EXPECTED LIFE YEARS	WEEKLY COST £
WINTER COAT	1 - 2	16 - 30	1 - 2	0.570
SUMMER COAT	1	10 - 15	1 - 2	0.280
TRACK-SUIT	1 - 2	10- 20	1 - 2	0.570
JEANS	0 - 2	9 - 10	1 - 1.5	0.340
SHORTS	3 - 4	3 - 5	1 - 1.5	0.280
T-SHIRT	4 - 6	4 - 5	1	0.570
BEST TROUSER	1	10 - 18	1	0.340
BEST SHIRT	1	7 - 13	1	0.250
BEST JUMPER	1	5 - 14	1 - 2	0.26
SWEAT-SHIRT	2	5 - 6	1 - 1.5	0.045
SWIMSUIT	1	5 - 10	1 - 2	0.048
BOXERS/ BRIEFS	5 - 7	1 - 2	.5 - 1	0.192
VESTS	0 - 2	0 - 2	1 - 1.5	0.192
PYJAMAS	0 - 2	0 - 6	1 - 3	0.230
DRESSING GOWN	0 - 2	0 - 2	.5 - 1	0.173
WINTER SOCKS	5 - 7	1 - 1.5	.5 - 1	0.270

SUMMER SOCKS	5 - 6	1 - 2	.5 - 1	0.270
WINTER JUMPERS	2 - 3	6 - 8	.5 - 2	0.340
WINTER HAT	1	3 - 4	2 - 3	0.038
SCARF	1	3 - 5	2 - 3	0.038
GLOVES	1	2 - 5	2	0.028
SHOES	1 - 2	5 - 12	.25 - 1	0.064
TRAINERS	1	5 - 6	.25 - 1	0.380
CANVAS PUMPS	1	2 - 4	.5 - 1	0.011
WELLING-TONS	1	7 - 8	1	0.153
SLIPPERS	1 - 2	3 - 5	1	0.5
SHIRT SCHOOL	2 - 4	3 - 5	.5 - 1	0.46
PULL-OVER	1 - 3	7 - 12	.5 - 1	0.040
SHORTS	1 - 2	2 - 5	1	0.028
T-SHIRT	1 - 2	3 - 6	1	0.153
GYM-SHOES	1	2 - 6	1	0.153

If a comparison is made of estimated lifespans of clothing and footwear items from different budget standards, it can be seen that adult respondents obtain a greater length of life from their clothing than do children. The following New York City Council and Montreal budget standards were based on an employed man's clothing, the clothing estimate used for comparison was from a male respondent whose estimates were typical for the sample.

Table 4.4
Comparison of male clothing estimate with New York and Montreal budget standards

Life spans in brackets are taken from the New York and Montreal budget standards 1982.

ITEM	NUMBER	COST	EXPECTED LIFE YEARS 92	(NY)	(Mon)	WEEKLY COST
Suit	0					
Trousers	2	15.00	4	(.3)	(.5)	0.14
Winter Coat	1	35.00	3	(2)	(4)	0.22
Shirts	7	5.99	2	(.4)	(.3)	0.40
Winter Sweater	2	17.99	4	(.3)	(2)	0.17
Leather Shoes	1	25.00	3	(.5)	(.5)	0.16

The difference in lifespans of articles varied between family members with adults generally obtaining more wear from their clothing. Children however obtained more wear from their footwear than the NY and Montreal budget standards suggested. The following table show the comparative differences in lifespans reported in this study and those of NY and Montreal budget standards:

Table 4.5
Comparisons of lifespans of selected items of children's clothing

Girl age 6-11	New York City	Montreal	Rowntree 92 (Mean)
Leather shoes	6 months	4months	8 months
Overcoat	3 years	2 years	15 months
Woollen sweater	1 year	2 years	1 year
Nightgown	1 year	2 years	1 year
Boy age 6-11			
Leather shoes	6 months	6 months	9 months
Overcoat	5 years	2 years	11 months
Woollen sweater	1 year	2 years	13 months
Shirt	6 months	6 months	1 year
Trousers	6 months	1 year	10 months
Pyjamas	6 months	2 years	10 months

The table raises some interesting points. Firstly overcoats given a lifespan of five years would seem an incredibly long durability period in view of the rate of growth of children during the ages of six to eleven. The coat would have to have been purchased extremely large at age six for it to last through to age eleven. Perhaps the coat was meant to be passed down to other children but this is presumptuous on the family having same sex children. The lifespan of overcoats for this sample ranged from 15 months for girls to only 11 months for boys. This lifespan would probably be commensurate with the quality of clothing purchased and rates of growth, and more importantly, this is the actual experience of mothers who cannot afford to be extravagant with their children's clothing. The lifespan given for shoes is half as much longer than for the NY and Montreal lifespans. It would seem that parents have to make their own clothing last longer in order to keep up with the needs of their children. It is documented that the expenditure on clothing and footwear for this family type increased from the previous year, yet within the lowest income band specified in Family Spending (92), clothing expenditure decreased from the previous year. Along with food, clothing seems to be another vital commodity which has to be cut back on in hard times. Many of the respondents did not include items of clothing in their lists which 'experts' would reasonably deem as essential by 1992 standards. Most of the women interviewed revealed that their partners did not wear nor possess a pair of pyjamas, they did not know how much they would cost if they needed a pair urgently; neither did many men or women include the cost of a winter coat or mackintosh in their estimates. This was correspondent with the findings of the survey conducted in Liverpool. (Liverpool City Council 1991) The survey found that 32% of poor people interviewed said they could not afford a warm waterproof coat and a staggering 74% could not afford new clothing. Nationally the picture is similar with the NCH survey reporting that 19% of families on low income saying that if they were to receive an extra £10 weekly, it would be spent on clothing. In the case of emergency, some said that if they needed to be admitted to hospital, they would borrow a pair of pyjamas from a relative or use the hospital supplies. Some items of clothing were purchased with the proviso that the garment be should suitable clothing as to be worn by both the husband and wife, as in the case of jeans, sweatshirts and tee-shirts. Clearly this situation should cause concern in 1992 when families cannot afford a basic decent wardrobe, when families are sharing clothes, where relatives are now relied upon to clothe children, where in the winter months many are forced to wear inferior and inadequate clothing simply because they cannot afford to purchase decent warm clothing.

Of the families interviewed, estimates within the ranges indicated above were obtained for twelve men, fifteen women and twenty children. The estimates were averaged for each member of the family as shown in the next table:

Table 4.6
Minimum clothing estimates 1992

Member	Man	Woman	Child 1	Child 2	Total
	£6.49	£5.92	£7.42	£6.17	£26.00

The total was then further reduced to take into account the school grants (in theory, if not always in practice) awarded to Income Support families. The total weekly cost of a primary poverty clothing budget amounted to £24.34 for a family of four.

mackintosh in their estimates. This was corroborated with the findings of the survey conducted in Liverpool (Liverpool City Council 1991). The survey found that 32% of poor people interviewed said they could not afford a warm waterproof coat and a staggering 74% could not afford new clothing. Nationally the picture is similar with the NCH survey reporting that 19% of [illegible]

[illegible]

[illegible]

5 Personal and household sundries

In his first major piece of research in 1899, Rowntree introduced his approach to calculating the sundries component of his primary poverty line. A family of average size used, he reckoned, about 1.51bs of soap per week at 3d. per lb. He found that information on the average sum required for other household necessaries very difficult to obtain. His inquiries about these were usually answered by some such remark as: 'if we have to buy anything extra, such as pots or pans, we have to spend less on food, that's all.' He thus, apparently arbitrarily, allowed 2d. per head per week (10d. for a family of five) to cover all household sundries, other than clothes and fuel. (p. 109) Rowntree gave no explanation as to how he arrived at this figure. This estimate did not allow anything for travelling, recreation or luxuries of any kind, or for sick and funeral clubs. It was presented to suffice only for the bare necessaries of merely physical efficiency in times of health. (p. 110) It allowed for items such as: washing and cleaning materials, renewals of linen, pots and pans.

Household sundries: His approach in gathering facts for this area of need was explained as being similar to the case of clothing and fuel - i.e., by interviewing working class women. Their replies varied within narrow limits and he decided to allow 1s./8d. a week as the necessary minimum expenditure for a family of five persons. (pp. 97/8)

Personal sundries: And for this component, he explained at length that he was forced to rely largely upon his own judgement, since, he reckoned, it was far less easy to fix a standard for such items as beer and tobacco, amusements and holidays, than it was for clothing and fuel. There were certain personal expenses which, he thought, might be regarded as compulsory, such as unemployment and health insurance contributions, sick clubs and trade union subscriptions, travelling to and from work, for which he allowed one shilling a week. Apart from these, 'we enter a field where judgement as to the sums which should be allowed when fixing a minimum cost of living is more difficult.' He interviewed a number of men whose expenditure on personal sundries varied substantially - from 6s./11d. a week in a case of a man with three dependent children, 'who is extraordinarily economical, and neither smokes nor drinks, and has no wireless set', to 20s./5d. for a man with two dependent children. Rowntree's conclusion was that nine shillings a week was the lowest sum that he could have included in his budget for personal sundries. In order that a judgement could be made as to whether this allowance was liberal or otherwise, he went on to catalogue a list of items which this sum could buy:

Unemployment and Health Insurance - 1s./7d.;
Contribution to sick and burial club - 1 shilling;
Trade Union subscription - 6d;
Travelling to and from work - 1 shilling;
Such necessaries as stamps, writing-paper etc. for the family - 6d;
A daily newspaper 7d;
Wireless - 6d;
All else: beer, tobacco, holidays, books, travelling etc. - 3s./4d.;
Total: Nine shillings.

Of course, this was offered merely as a typical way of spending money. Rowntree acknowledged that men spend more or less on different items according to their personal inclinations. He also drew attention to the very small margin which there he left for optional expenditure. The total available was only 4s./11d. a week, and out of this, certain expenditure could not be avoided, e.g. stamps, writing paper, haircutting for the family etc., which he estimated at 6d. a week altogether. There were other expenses which, though not absolutely essential, could not be regarded as extravagant, e.g. a daily newspaper 7d., and wireless set 6d., together 1s./1d. After all the above had been provided for, there remained a mere 3s./4d. a week for <u>all else</u> - beer, tobacco, presents for the children, holidays, bus rides, all travelling except that of the father to and from work, books and all amusements such as cinemas, football matches etc. 'When I consider how stringent must be the economy in these things if the expenditure on the physical necessities of physical efficiency is not to be entrenched upon, I am almost ashamed to put forward so low an estimate for personal sundries as nine shillings a week. I refrain from raising it however, for two reasons: first I am aware that the period of stringency lasts only for so long as there are three dependent children; and second that I want to make my figure of the human needs of labour one which is unassailable.' (pp. 98/101) For personal sundries, Rowntree allowed for most of the items included in our 1992 budget - and indeed, perhaps given that the current study did not allow for alcohol or tobacco at all, Rowntree's 1899 allowances were relatively more generous than the budgets offered here.

Again turning to the needs of women in this area, Rowntree allowed 7s./6d. a week (including compulsory contributions to health and unemployment insurance (1s./3d. a week), Trade Union subscriptions, annual holidays and sundries). These estimates also included: hospital contributions, sick club, travelling to and from work, sports club subscriptions, amusements and charity, haircutting and other sundries.

Once more, masterfully preempting the inevitable criticism which he knew would be levelled against any 'slackness' in his calculations of 'physical efficiency' needs, he wrote: 'Doubtless, the first reaction of some of my readers to what I have said will be that it is not in accord with the facts. They will say that families of five with wages no higher than my minimum do found quite a bit of money each week for "luxuries". The men smoke quite a lot of cigarettes and drink quite a few glasses of beer, and then look at the cinemas. Crowded with working people every day. Yes, all that is true, but so are my facts and figures. The explanation is that working people are just as human as those with more money. They cannot live on just a "fodder basis". They crave for relaxation and recreation just as we do. (But) they pay dearly for their pleasures', (by going without necessities). (pp. 126/7). He continued calculations in this area of need in 1941:

Personal sundries consisted of:
Unemployment & health insurance - 1s./7d.;
Stamps, writing-paper etc. - 6d;
Contribution to sick and burial club - 1 shilling;
Daily newspaper - 7d;
Trade Union subscriptions - 6d;
Wireless - 6d;
Travelling to and from work - 1 shilling;
All else: beer, tobacco, presents, holidays, books, travelling etc. 3s./4d.:
TOTAL - 9 shillings (p. 28)

Rowntree allowed for variations in the sums required for differently constituted families and based these upon careful examination of the families' needs. He gave the following example: a man and woman without children were allowed one shilling for household sundries, the first and second child 2d. each, the third and subsequent children 4d. each. Consideration of what was comprised under the heading 'Household Sundries' demonstrated that this division was more accurate than if a uniform allowance had been made for household sundries for every member of the family. A detailed examination showed that the minimum figure he could allow for household sundries for a man, woman and three children was 1s./8d. He clearly could not assume that the necessary expenditure on household sundries for a single person would only amount to one-fifth of this, because the home must still be kept in order, no matter how the family was constituted. So he allowed 9d. for a single man or woman, and one shilling where two persons were living together. The addition of one or two children did not, he reckoned, involve a pro-rata increase in the sum needed for household sundries and therefore only 2d. was allowed for each of the first two children. That brought the average amount per person allowed for household sundries to 4d, and this amount per head was added for any further children or other dependents. Where the parents were 'young', an allowance was made for necessary saving: five shillings a week was allowed for a young married man with one child and three shillings for a man with two children. The item for savings was included in the necessary expenditure in the case of young married couples, 'for it is a rare occurrence for a young couple to start their married life with a house so fully furnished as to meet even the minimum requirements of a family. My cost of living standard only allows for the maintenance of a fully furnished house. It allows nothing for the purchase of furniture and bedding, or for other similar expenditure of a non-recurring nature.' (p. 31)

In the examination of household sundries in 1950, Rowntree and Laver concluded that a man, woman and three children should be allowed six shillings. No explanation as to how Rowntree arrived at this figure was offered. The question of how to divide this amount for families of different compositions was addressed: 'Some items of expenditure will not be affected to any significant extent by the size of the family (e.g. dust pans, pails, sweeping brushes), others will vary to a certain extent (e.g. sheets, towels, crockery and household soap), and the expenditure on other items will vary strictly in accordance with the number of members in the family (e.g. toothbrushes, toilet soap etc.) Clearly it is impossible to get a mathematically accurate figure showing the amount to allow for families of different sizes ... we ... allow the following sums for families of different sizes:

No. of persons	Amount allowed for household sundries per week
1	2/5
2	3/10
3	5/-
4	5/8
5	6/-
6	6/4
7	6/8

This was an estimate only. In the case of food, clothing and fuel and light, he could give precise figures, but the total amount involved for household sundries was only six shillings, which was a small proportion of the total expenditure and therefore any inaccuracy there may have been in the division of household sundries for families of different sizes was deemed relatively unimportant. (pp. 17/18)

And for personal sundries, up to that point, their estimates about the necessary expenditure on food, clothing, household sundries, fuel and lighting were based on 'carefully ascertained facts', but in the matter of expenditure on personal sundries, they were obliged very largely to rely on their own judgement in deciding what items to include. (p. 22) When Rowntree and Laver compared their 1950 measurements to 1936 list of personal sundries, they commented that, as the payment of Unemployment and Health Insurance was then compulsory, these (and any Income Tax payable) were deducted from wages in the figures showing the workers' earnings and therefore they did not appear under the heading of personal sundries. Although the statutory benefits under the Health Scheme were, at that stage, more liberal than they were, payment to a sick club was still necessary for, of course, the statutory benefit fell much below the normal earnings of men and women at work. Payments to a burial club were also usual notwithstanding the death grant of £20 for an adult and grants which varied from £5 to £15 according to age of children under 18. A funeral in 1950, as with today, was a very expensive affair: 'Working people make great sacrifices to ensure their dead are buried with due respect. We therefore include one shilling for expenditure on sick and burial clubs.' In the case of men, they increased the figure for the expenditure on Trade Union subscriptions from 6d to 9d. They did not alter the cost of travelling to and from work, but they doubled the sum allowed for stamps, writing-paper etc. In view of increases in the postage rates and the cost of other items coming under this heading, they added 1d to the cost of a daily newspaper as Sunday newspapers then cost 2d. They also doubled the amount allowed for 'All Else': 'Even this sum will not buy anything like as much as 3s./4d. did in 1936. These modifications increase the sum allowed for personal sundries for a family of five from 9s. (in 1936) to 11s./6d., assuming that the man is in employment.' His personal sundries budget was made up as follows:

	s/d
Contribution to sick and burial club	9d
Trade Union subscription	1s
Travelling to and from work	1s
Stamps, writing-paper etc	1s
Daily newspaper	8d
Wireless	5d

(This was 1d less than 1936 as in 1950, comparatively few people had to buy batteries. The small amount for electricity for a wireless set was included in the expenditure on fuel and light).

All else: beer, tobacco, presents, holidays, books, travelling etc. 6s8d

TOTAL 11s8d

If the man and woman were both working, the figure allowed for personal sundries was increased by 1s 6d - 1s. for travelling to and from work for the woman and 6d for her Trade Union subscriptions. If the chief wage earner was a woman, the allowance of 6/8 for 'All else' would have been reduced to 5s and the Trade Union subscription from 9d to 6d. In the case of unemployed persons, they deducted the Trade Union subscription, because on the schedules, almost all of those who were unemployed were sick and had been unemployed for a very long time. They also deducted the 1s for travelling to and from work. (pp. 22/24)

In 1936, Rowntree made an allowance of 5s. a week for a young married couple and one child, 3s. for a married couple with two children. In view of the increased cost of living, he allowed 10s. for a young couple with one child and 6s. if there were two children. It was necessary to fix arbitrarily the age at which married couples cease to be 'young' for the purpose of his allowance and he decided that it should be the 30th birthday of the chief wage-earner. (p. 25)

The team involved in constructing the personal and household sundries budget for 1992 included clothing experts and home economists, whose task was to 'step into Rowntree's shoes' and try to imagine what he would have included in his primary poverty line, to cost the items and produce a minimum budget standard. This budget proved to be the most problematic to construct. The task for the team included making subjective yet informed decisions on which items should be included in the 1992 budget, produce costings and life spans. This component of the household/personal sundries budget was extremely complex as it covered many areas of household expenditure. These included first aid and medical needs, personal cleanliness and sundries items. The household section included furnishings, textiles, white goods, hardware, stationery products, cleaning materials, household services, leisure goods and activities and transport costs. In order to create a minimum needs budget the team used a number of research projects as reference points with which to create the primary lists. (NFCA 1992, Stitt 1989, FBU WP 1992) These lists were then circulated to the team members and home economists within the University. Each list was discussed and assessed and amended in line with the informed opinion of each of the experts. They each made their own professional judgements (as Rowntree had done) on what they believed to be a minimum requirement for 1992 based on their own expertise. The original estimates derived from the primary lists came to £47.21, costed at 1990 prices; they were then upgraded to the 1992 costings of £51.08. The changes made to each individual list by the experts reduced the final costs to £47.07. The exclusion of alcohol and tobacco was made in the knowledge that many people cope with everyday stresses with smoking and drinking and in no way should their exclusion be misinterpreted as prescriptive or judgmental, but rather in the spirit of Rowntree's objective of pre-empting criticism.

As could be imagined, the process of reduction (or increase) was one fraught with professional and personal dilemmas, involving experts making value judgements on the needs of poor families and as such, they were conscious of the inevitable criticisms they would encounter. But the process of debate was necessary in devising an irreducible budget for 1992; fear of criticism would not help the debate. Rowntree himself had sought constructive opinions of his budgets. Similarly during the compilation of the data, the team took their preliminary costings to various academic conferences to 'air' their findings and this proved to be both constructive and informative and contributed to the final modifications which the team believed strengthened the study.

Although each of the areas of the household budget received minor modifications, it was leisure goods and services which seemed to dominate the debate. This list included a television set, video recorder, a small selection of games for children and entertainments. The inclusion of a video recorder was questioned by some members of the team as an unnecessary expenditure, whilst others felt that peer group pressure placed on children should be a consideration; by not including a video recorder would reinforce the feelings of disadvantage felt by these children who were already receiving free school meals and clothing grants. Some described the ownership of a video as essential, in view of the limited scope within the income for any other source of entertainment. The cost of a week's holiday at a holiday camp during the cheaper end of the children's statutory summer holiday was also questioned, as it was believed that a holiday could be forfeited in favour of extra expenditure on something deemed more essential; others felt that a holiday was absolutely crucial for the integrative development of the family and would be an essential break away from the grind of everyday life. Indeed, it was argued that poor families are in greater need of an away-from-home holiday than better-off families because of the need to have even a brief respite from the daily, even hourly grind of a life of struggle, sometimes hopelessness. The cost of indoor swimming was also debated; some felt that a weekly session was too often, others felt it was necessary for the physical well being of all the family. Only one trip to the cinema yearly was included, and felt by some to be rather miserly.

Rowntree had included the cost of basic furniture for younger households who were building up their home. (p. 31) The 1992 study included these costs in the face of criticism from those who felt that most families already possessed basic items. The rationale for their inclusion was simple: all household goods need replacing at some time - even the government acknowledges this need, as the Social Fund budgeting loan scheme was designed to meet 'the important intermittent expenses...for which it may be difficult to budget'. The lifespans used for larger items would mean perhaps that over a period of time, these items would only need replacing once or twice, but they **would** eventually need replacing. This was factually substantiated by one of the mothers interviewed, who had made a request to the DSS for a Social Fund loan for the purchase of a washing machine. She was refused, on the grounds that she had an immersion heater for hot water and a veranda on which to dry the clothes. The cost of a new machine was out of the question; her previous washing machine was bought secondhand and lasted only three years. She felt it was false economy buying secondhand. They also pointed out to her that she had an outstanding loan for a telephone installation which she needed due to her son's medical condition which often required urgent attention. When she had originally applied for this loan they had classed it as a luxury even though she had produced medical documentation in support of her case. In effect she felt they were refusing her a loan for a washing machine because she was already in debt to the department. They were asserting that the family could not afford to accommodate extra payments out of their already strained income. The woman argued that the costs involved in washing and drying at the local launderette were in excess of those she would have to repay out of her income for a loan, with no washing machine at the end of it.

The question of new versus secondhand was debated amongst the experts, with calculation of costs and lifespans of items of unknown age and quality creating obvious problems. In order to define a minimum budget, both old and new types of furniture were costed and assigned appropriate lifespans. As expected there was virtually no difference found between the weekly costs. There were problems in attributing costs for secondhand quality goods or furniture from which one may expect a lifetime of service and the cheap alternative of essentially a lower quality and shorter lifespan. What had emerged from the study was that the choice of whether to buy secondhand versus new was not an option open to many of the families because, generally secondhand dealers required cash payment. It was the case that some of the sample could only afford to make their large purchases through weekly instalments from mail order catalogues. This study found, as Rowntree had, that the women interviewed were extremely adept at managing their incomes, their knowledge of budgeting for needs was far more acute and pertinent to their situation than the knowledge of those whose job it was to administer the welfare funds.

The PSI report found that budgets of low income households were not stretching to meet basic items, that when people were asked if there was anything they really needed but they could not afford, 14% said clothing, 4% could not afford food and the following list, of particular interest for this component of the budget, were items felt to be really needed but which could not be afforded:

Decorating or home repairs	34%
Presents for the family	23%
A holiday or family outing	23%
Large items of home equipment	18%

People with less than £100 per week reported an average of almost three times as many unmet needs as people with more than £400.(p.25)

This component also needed to include costings for transport, no allowance was made for the running costs of a car and the cheapest form of local transport on Merseyside was by bus. The question of how many trips need to be made weekly was pondered and as was who would make them. Obviously the answers would be arbitrary at this stage but they should be seen to be of a subsistence nature. It was decided that only one trip per person could be accommodated within the budget and this was achieved by using the local save-away tickets, which are valid for one day off-peak only or all day over the weekends. For a family of two adults and two children one trip or visit out weekly by this method would cost £4.90. By only including one trip, this reinforced the cautious nature of the budget standard set.

It became apparent that a consensus of opinion could not be reached for a definitive budget for this particular component. Therefore the re-adjusted estimates pruned from the primary lists were aggregated to arrive at the final estimate of the personal and household sundries budget. They had then undergone a process of investigation and debate until the final estimates were arrived at, and lastly the costs were updated to 1992. In order to give the reader a fuller representation of what life on a minimum income in 1992 entails, it is important to emphasise some of the items not included in the primary lists. The costs of hire and charges for a telephone were not included, even though the use of a 'phone could be regarded as an asset now that claimants are compelled to demonstrate evidence that they are 'actively seeking work' in order to remain entitled to welfare payments. No allowance for gifts or Xmas or birthday presents was allowed. Blank audio tapes were included in the budget, as the purchase of original material was not. No allowances for magazines, good quality newspapers, nor materials associated with hobbies or pastimes, (ie. gardening, photography etc) were allowed. There was nothing in this budget which permitted paid entry to sports venues, football matches, keep-fit clubs or social clubs. This elimination of choice also extended to children's ability to join clubs or participate in activities which required some financial outlay, i.e., dancing lessons, ju-jitsu, disco's, karate, scouts, guides - the list is endless.

The lack of adequate income effectively discriminates certain children from taking part in the normal everyday activities in which their friends may be able to participate in. This deterioration of standards for children has been an issue which could be addressed within the UN convention on the 'Rights of the Child'. Just taking the social development of the children as an example highlights that as a society, rather than improving conditions for children, the situation is such that in the UK in 1992, children are becoming more and more impoverished. Under Article 27 of the UN convention on the rights of a child, the child has the 'right to physical, mental and social development' and under Article 11, the treaty stresses the 'continuous improvement of living conditions and the right to the highest possible level of health'. (Van Beuren G, CPAG Annual Conference 1992) From the estimates given here, it is clear that children from low income families are being deprived of even the most basic necessities.

Water clearly is essential to the physical well being of an individual, disconnection could lead to increased illness and spread of disease. Recent evidence has emerged that where disconnections have risen, so too have the incidence of certain diseases: '..there is a direct association between both diseases and poverty. Families who are poor, and are more likely to be at risk of having their water cut off, are also at most risk of being cut off.'(Sandwell Health Authority, Feb. 1993, personal communication) In view of the important health aspect, the inclusion of water rates is deemed to be an essential component of the Rowntree budget. Adults on Income support are allowed discount on their payments of Poll Tax of 80%, however they have to pay the other 20% out of their benefit, failure to pay up can result in the payments being deducted at source, fines seizure of possessions and/or imprisonment. The CAB in Liverpool in 1992 compiled a profile of the problems brought to them by clients. Of these, 44.3% were in arrears for their water supply to the extent that they were at risk of disconnection. The figure for the Poll Tax was a massive 76.7%. (Personal communication)

As the study was conducted in Liverpool the team used the local community charge rates for the area. The annual charge for 1992/3 was £398 p.a., 20% of which amounts to £1.53 weekly for each adult in the household. In our typical family this amounts to a weekly outlay of £3.06. Water rates were more difficult to assess as the calculation included taking into account many variables such as housing type, location and rateable value. Since the abolition of the rates system, houses built since have either been metered or have been assigned an arbitrary rateable value on which to base their water rates, based on the similarity of location and housing size to other housing in the area. A spokesperson for North West Water informed us that the average rateable value in and around the city of Liverpool was generally £200 p.a., lower graded properties in poorer areas could be rated at £98 p.a. The calculation of water rates dependent on rateable value still exists for the vast majority of householders and is calculated thus:

	Rateable Value(£) x .272p	=	water services
+	Rateable Value(£) x .476p	=	sewerage charges
+	Standing Charge	=	£25 p.a.

In view of the difference of the properties of the householders taking part in this study, it was decided to set an arbitrarily low rateable value based on the midpoint between the average and the low rateable value (£149) and apply the criteria for assessing the water rate, which amounted to £2.62 weekly.

The final estimate for this section can be summarised as follows;

Household/Personal sundries		£47.07
Poll Tax (2 adults)		3.06
Water rates (RV £149)		2.62
	TOTAL	52.75

Table 5.1 (overleaf) is an entire catalogue of all the items agreed upon under the personal and household sundries component of our 1992 primary poverty line:

Table 5.1
Items, costs and lifespans of the household sundries element of the 1992 primary poverty line.

PERSONAL CARE	Initial cost £	Lifespan years	Weekly cost (pence)
First aid kit	12.99	2	0.134
other items			0.275
		TOTAL	0.400
PERSONAL CLEANLINESS			
Toilet soap (30 tablets)	15.55	1	0.299
Toothpaste (13)	14.87	1	0.286
Toothbrushes (4)	3.00	3months	0.230
Hairbrushes (2)	4.00	2	0.038
Combs (2)	2.00	2	0.019
Shampoo (24)	47.97	1	0.919
Sanitary protection	1.55	1month	0.358
Razor and Blades	7.07	1	0.136
Shaving Foam (4)	3.95	1	0.076
Nail Clippers	0.99	3	0.006
Deodorant 1	1.45	6months	0.006
Haircuts 2 Adults		3months	2.001
Haircuts 2 Children		4months	0.580
		TOTAL	4.954
PERSONAL SUNDRIES			
Toilet bag (1)	2.15	3	0.014
Handbag (1)	14.99	5	0.058
Purse (1)	6.99	5	0.027
Wallet (1)	5.99	5	0.023
School bags (2)	11.24	2	0.108
Ladies watch	24.99	10	0.048
Gents watch	27.45	10	0.053
Shaving mirror	3.60	5	0.014
Clocks	22.25	5	0.086
Holdalls	24.70	5	0.095

		TOTAL	0.524

COSMETICS/AFTERSHAVE

Foundation	2.60	1	0.050
Blusher	2.75	1	0.053
Eyeshadow	2.70	1	0.052
Mascara	2.50	1	0.048
Lipstick	2.30	6months	0.088
Aftershave	3.50	6months	0.135
Hand/body lotion	2.05	6months	0.079
Cosmetic bag	3.25	3	0.021
		TOTAL	0.526

HOUSEHOLD GOODS AND SERVICES

	Initial Cost £	Lifespan years	Weekly Cost (pence)
Three seater settee	349.95	15	0.449
Armchair (2)	391.90	15	0.502
Bookshelf (1)	29.99	20	0.029
Chairs (4)	48.00	15	0.061
Dining table	99.99	15	0.128
Double wardrobe	99.99	20	0.192
Chest of drawers (2)	169.90	20	0.163
Double divan (1)	249.95	15	0.320
Single divan (2)	320.00	15	0.410
Single wardrobes (2)	132.98	20	0.127
		TOTAL	2.381

FLOORCOVERINGS

Hall, stairs and Landing	293.58	7	0.807
Underlay	56.27	14	0.077
Fitting	Free		
Lounge	258.74	7	0.711
Underlay	64.91	14	0.089
Fitting	Free		
Kitchen			
Vinyl tiles	140.42	7	0.386

Bathroom	72.62	7	0.199
Bedroom	183.74	7	0.504
Bedroom	81.60	5	0.314
Bedroom	80.77	7	0.222
		TOTAL	3.309

	Initial Cost £	Lifespan years	Weekly Cost (pence)
CURTAINS			
Kitchen/living room	23.99	8	0.058
Living room	89.98	12	0.144
Living room nets	15.80	8	0.038
Bathroom	24.99	8	0.060
Bedroom 1	29.99	8	0.072
Bedroom 2	13.99	8	0.034
Bedroom 3	13.99	8	0.034
		TOTAL	0.440

HOUSEHOLD TEXTILES			
Pillows 4	10.00	8	0.019
Double quilt cover & pillow cases 2	39.98	8	0.096
Single quilt cover 2 Pillow cases 4	44.00	5	0.169
Double fitted sheet2	23.98	6	0.077
Single fitted sheet4	39.96	4	0.288
Double quilt 1	39.99	10	0.077
Single quilt 2	59.98	8	0.144
Flannels 4	4.00	1	0.076
Hand towels 4	11.96	5	0.046
Medium towels 2	11.98	5	0.046
Bath towels 4	31.96	7	0.087
Tea towels 5	5.00	3	0.032
Bath mat	8.99	6	0.029
Table cloth	17.99	6	0.057
		TOTAL	1.24

GAS/ELECTRICAL APPLIANCES

Fridge	169.99	15	0.218
Gas cooker	299.99	12	0.346
Kettle	13.95	8	0.034
Washing machine	389.99	10	0.750
Hair dryer	8.95	5	0.034
Iron	23.99	8	0.058
Vacuum cleaner	109.99	10	0.212
Accessories			.377
Repairs, washing machine	87.50	10	0.318
Repairs, gas cooker	65.00	12	0.104
Repairs, vacuum cleaner	45.00	10	0.087
		TOTAL	2.612

HARDWARE/OTHER APPLIANCES

Crockery set	43.98	10	0.085
Mugs	9.98	5	0.038
Teapot	5.95	7	0.016
Oven dish set	9.99	10	0.019
Cruet	7.99	10	0.015
Egg cups	7.99	10	0.015
Tumblers	3.99	5	0.004
Glass bowl set	3.99	10	0.008
Measuring jug	6.58	5	0.024
Large mixing bowl	6.58	5	0.024
Utensil set	9.49	10	0.018
Tin opener	0.75	2	0.007
Cutlery set	44.00	8	0.105
Scissors	7.99	10	0.015
Wooden spoon set	1.50	5	0.006
Potato peeler	1.15	1	0.022
Balloon whisk	2.49	5	0.010
Cheese grater	3.99	10	0.008
Chopping board	2.25	5	0.009
Cookware set	9.99	10	0.019
Pastry cutters	1.99	10	0.004
Cooling rack	2.50	10	0.005
Rolling pin	2.99	15	0.004
Sieve	4.99	15	0.006
Saucepan set	39.99	15	0.051

Milk pan	5.95	15	0.008
Colander	2.99	5	0.012
Kitchen scales	5.99	10	0.012
Oven gloves	1.75	2	0.017
Plastic food box(2)	2.50	10	0.010
Vacuum flask	4.75	10	0.009
Mop	3.95	10	0.008
Mop head	1.95	1	0.038
Dustpan & brush	2.50	10	0.005
Shoe brushes	2.78	5	0.011
Washing up bowl	2.65	5	0.010
Swing bin	8.95	10	0.017
Batteries			0.017
Candles	.96	2	0.009
Freezer containers	1.78	1	0.034
Cling film	2.16	1	0.042
Foil	3.99	1	0.077
Ironing board	19.99	10	0.038
Ironing board cover	2.25	1	0.043
Clothes airer	13.99	15	0.018
Washing line	1.10	10	0.038
Clothes pegs	3.45	5	0.013
Prop	4.29	10	0.008
Coat hangers	5.00	10	0.010
Childs PVC apron	2.45	3	0.015
Table mat set	14.99	10	0.029
Plug in fluorescent light	15.99	8	0.038
Lampshades (3)	21.97	8	0.053
Smoke detector	8.99	10	0.017
Torch	2.99	10	0.006
Hand shears	9.99	25	0.008
Screw drivers	2.45	15	0.003
Claw hammer	6.99	15	0.009
Spanner set	9.99	20	0.010
Pliers	6.29	20	0.006
Safety knife	3.99	20	0.004
Nails	0.99	2	0.010
Steel rule	2.09	15	0.003
Paint brushes (4)	9.16	5	0.036
Ladder	29.99	20	0.029
Wallpaper/paint	50.00	1.5	0.641
		TOTAL	2.225

	Initial cost £	Lifespan years	Weekly cost (pence)
Stationary and paper goods			1.50
Cleaning products			2.90
HOUSEHOLD SUNDRIES			
Contents Insurance			1.260
Postage 52/1st class			0.220
129/2nd class			0.422
Parcel post x 2(yearly)			0.076
Shoe repairs			0.415
Telephone calls (36/call box)			0.069
Dry cleaning			0.258
Boys football club membership @ £2 yr			0.038
Life insurance cover (adults only)			2.00
		TOTAL	9.16
LEISURE GOODS AND SERVICES			
Television	219.99	12	0.353
Radio/cassette player	39.50	10	0.076
AV repairs/maintenance			1.189
Blank audio tapes (5)	9.99	4	0.192
Pack cards	0.99	5	0.008
Scrabble	7.50	10	0.014
Monopoly	7.50	10	0.014
Games compendium	8.75	8	0.021
Calender	2.99	1	0.058
Map A-Z	2.85	4	0.014
Address book	2.25	4	0.011
Diary	2.15	1	0.041
Dictionary	5.95	10	0.011
Cookery book	9.95	10	0.013
Encyclopedia	10.99	10	0.021
Bible	7.50	20	0.007
Seasonal items			0.572

	Initial Cost £	Lifespan years	Weekly Cost (pence)
Daily newspaper			1.500
Sunday newspaper			0.550
Local newspaper			0.250
TV licence			0.500
School trips (primary)			0.550
(secondary)			0.550
School craft costs(primary)			0.058
(secondary)			0.058
School musical			0.012
Visit to cinema	10.00	1	0.190
Indoor swimming	4.30	52	4.300
Family holiday	175.00	1	3.365
		TOTAL	14.38
Transport costs	4.90	52	4.90
		TOTAL	£47.07

6 The 1992 Rowntree primary poverty line

By adding up the various items of necessary expenditure under the main headings in 1899, Rowntree (pp.109/110), presented his aggregate primary poverty line as follows:

Table 6.1

Minimum necessary weekly expenditure for various family types in 1899

Family	Food	Rent	Household Sundries	Total
1 man	3s.}	1/6	2/6	7s.
1 woman	3s.}	each	2/6	7s.
1 man,1 woman				
	6s.}		3/2	11/9
	}	2/6		
1 man,1 woman +				
1 child	8/3}		3/9	14/6
2 children	10/6}		4/4	18/10
	}	4s.		
3 children	12/9}		4/11	21/8
4 children	15s.}	5/6		26s.

5 children	17/3}		6/1	28/10
	}	5/6		
6 children	19/6}		6/8	31/8
7 children	21/9}		7/3	34/6
8 children	24s.}		7/10	37/4

Rowntree could claim, under the ultimate test, in 1903 that: 'Even she (Mrs. Bosanquet of the Charity Organisation Society) can find no fault with my allowance of 6d. a week to keep an adult in boots and clothes, 1s./10d. per week per family for coal and 2d. per week per head to cover all other expenditure including lighting, soap, household replacements, purchase of new furniture etc.' (Rowntree 1903, p. 20)

Doing the same in 1941, the following table shows the sums necessary to enable families of different sizes and differently constituted to live at the same standard of comfort as an urban family of man, woman, and three children, spending 43s./6d. a week (excluding rent):

Table 6.2
Minimum necessary weekly expenditure for various family types in 1941

	Employed	Unemployed	OAP
Man (alone)	25/10	22/9	15/3
Woman (alone)	21/3	17/6	12/6
Man & Woman	31/11	27/8	22/4
" " + 1 child	38/1	35s	-
" " + 2 children	41/2	38/8	-
" " + 3 children	43/6	40/5	-

Add 5/4 for each additional dependent child
Add 7/8 for an adult female dependent on the family
Add 11/5 " male "
Add 4/9 for an adult female paying board and lodgings
Add 5/9 " male "

(For unemployed men, deductions of 1s./7d. for health and unemployment insurance contributions, 6d. for Trade Union subscriptions, 1s. for travelling to and from work). (For unemployed women, deduction of 1s./3d. for health and unemployment insurance contributions, 6d. for Trade Union subscriptions, 1s. for travelling to and from work, and 1s. for personal sundries - these, for considered reasons, were allowed on a slightly more liberal scale for employed women than employed men and this additional sum was not considered necessary for a woman when unemployed). (The amount allowed for an OAP living with a family was 10s./5d. in the case of a man and 7s./8d. in that of a woman. The difference between the 11s./5d. for an adult dependent male and the 10s./5d. for an OAP was because the latter was allowed 1s. less for clothing). (The amounts for lodgers covered food and household sundries, all other living costs being met by the lodgers.) (p. 30)

At 1936 prices, the poverty line of 1899 would have been drawn at a family income of 30s./7d. for a family of five. Rowntree chose instead to set his new poverty line at 43s./6d. (after paying rent), again demonstrating his commitment to increasing the calculations of the subsistence needs of the poor in line with national economic progress. It would have been quite an easy task to take Rowntree's 1899 poverty line and up-date it in line with the Retail Price Index and expansion of Gross Domestic Product (to reflect national economic prosperity). (See Stitt 1992) However, the increases in Rowntree's poverty standards from 1899 to 1936/41 to 1950 reflect more factors and considerations than these. The task therefore for this study has been to drawing a 1992 primary poverty line in its own right and not simply to up-date Rowntree from 1899.

And finally, drawing together his 1950 poverty line, he added together the necessary weekly expenditure, excluding rent, under different headings for a family of five and arrived at a total of £5.0.2d made up as follows:

Table 6.3
Rowntree & Laver's 1950 poverty line

	Food	Clothing
Man	12/6½	6/1
Woman	10/5	5/2
3 children	£1-4-4½	16/6
	£2-7-4	£1-7-9
Household sundries		6s
Fuel and light		7/7
Personal sundries		11/6
Total..................................		£5-0-2. (p. 24)

Rowntree and Laver included other sources of income than wages - e.g. statutory welfare benefits, vegetables grown at home, free milk at school, cheap milk for infants etc. Rent and rates were deducted from income and the residual income was related to the poverty line. The following table shows the amount required for differently constituted families:

Table 6.4
Minimum necessary weekly expenditure for various family types in 1950

	Employed			Unemployed		
	£	s	d	£	s	d
Man alone	1	16	1	1	17	11
Woman alone	1	11	1	1	13	2
2 women living together	2	14	7	2	14	1
Man and woman	2	17	2	2	16	2
+ 1 child	3	11	11	3	10	11
+ 2 children	4	6	4	4	5	4
+ 3 children	5	0	2	4	19	2

(Add 14s for each additional dependent child
Add 15/111 " adult female
Add 19s " male
Add 10/9 " 1 adult female lodger*
Add 12/11 " male*
Add 23/8 " male & female lodger*
Add 8/3 " child lodger*
(*food and increment on household sundries only). (p. 28)

And finally, all that remains to be done in this section is to aggregate the estimates which we have presented so far to table the weekly minimum necessary expenditure for a family of four:

Table 6.5
Rowntree weekly poverty line for 1992

	£
Food	37.26
Fuel	15.43
Clothing	24.34
Personal & household sundries	47.07
Community charge	3.06
Water rates	2.15
Total	**129.31**

Current Income support levels for a family comprising two adults and two children of similar ages researched here would be:

	£
Couple (over 18)	66.60
Child (under age 11) 1	14.55
Child (under age 11) 2	14.55
Family Premium	9.30
Total	**105.00**

The level of Income Support in 1992 was almost £25 below the cost of a minimum subsistence standard of living for a family of adult male, adult female and two young children. Given the meagre, parsimonious and minimalist nature of the primary poverty line presented here, this is an unambiguous damning indictment of the level of 'safety net' provision in the poor relief system in Britain in the 1990s.

7 Numbers living in primary poverty

As Rowntree stated in Chapter 11 of the 1901 book, an estimate was made of the earnings of every working class family in York. So as to measure the numbers of these families who were living in a state of 'primary' poverty, the income of each was compared with the foregoing standard, due allowance being made in every case for size of family and rent paid. He found that no less than 1,465 families, comprising 7,230 persons were living in 'primary' poverty. **This was equal to 15.46% of the wage earning class in York and to 9.91% of the whole population of the city**. This estimate, it should be particularly noted, was based upon the assumption that **every penny earned by every member of the family went into the family purse** and was judiciously expended upon necessaries. (p. 111)

Going further into his findings, Rowntree continued to explain that, with a view of showing the number of persons but slightly above the 'primary' poverty line, he ascertained what would the total number below this line had the standard of necessary weekly family expenditure been increased by: (a) 2s. and; (b) by 6s. (This figure of 6s. had been selected with reference to the expenditure on alcohol which he referred to earlier in his book). The results are shown in Table 7.1: The data revealed in this table reflects the self-induced dilemma faced by policy-makers when debating setting a poverty line - the higher the poverty line, the greater the numbers of poor people, the greater the pressure to reduce the poverty line, particularly when this poverty line is associated with poor relief benefits. By raising his poverty standard by 6s. in 1899, Rowntree immediately more than doubled the numbers of poor. The following data should not be seen as Rowntree 'quantifying' the 'poor' - i.e., primary + secondary. The gap between both was largely a matter of opinion and involved much more than 'wasteful' expenditure on alcohol and tobacco.

Table 7.1
Numbers living below and marginally above the primary poverty line 1899

	No. of persons	% of Wage earning Class	% of Total Pop. of City
Persons below the primary poverty line	7230	15.46	9.91
Persons belonging to families whose total weekly earnings are either below or not more than 2s. above the 'primary' poverty line	9542	20.40	13.09
Persons belonging etc. ... 6s. ... below ... etc.	15727	33.63	21.50

(pp 111/2)

In 'Poverty and Progress', (1941) it was shown that 17,185 persons, equivalent to 31.1% of the working class population in York were living below the **minimum** standard. (p. 34) Here Rowntree was referring to the 'Poverty Line' - primary and secondary.

Whilst in 1899, of the working class population, 15.45% were living in primary poverty, by 1936, 6.8% of the working class population were living in primary poverty. In other words,

> the proportion of **the working class population living in abject poverty had been reduced by over one-half**'. (p. 451) Rowntree concluded: 'I suggest that we should probably not be very far wrong if we put the standard of living available to the workers in 1936 at about 30% higher

than it was in 1899.'

Three causes accounted for this increase: (1) a reduction in the size of the family; (2) the increase in real wages; (3) the remarkable growth in social services (poor relief). His inquiry showed that 31.1% of the working class population were in receipt of insufficient income to enable them to live in accordance with his minimum standard and so were classified as living under the poverty line. (pp. 453/456) Here again, Rowntree was referring to primary and secondary poverty. But he added his usual caveat: 'I must again warn the reader against drawing a completely false deduction from the fact that in 1899, I concluded that 33% of the working class population were living in poverty and ... I conclude that 31.1% are living in poverty through inadequate income and suggest that perhaps a further 7 - 10% may possibly be in this state through expenditure on non-essentials. In 1899, I estimated that 17.93% of the population were living in "secondary" poverty. The facts that, in 1899, only 33.39% of the working class was regarded as living in poverty, either primary or secondary, whereas, in 1936, 31.3% are living below the minimum through lack of income, and an unknown further proportion, possibly 7 10% are living in secondary poverty, have therefore no relation to each other. The only figures that are absolutely comparable are those for primary poverty and as we have seen, the proportion of the working class population living in primary poverty in 1936 was 6.8%, whereas, in 1899, it was 15.46%.' (pp. 460/1)

His 1936 study showed that primary poverty fell from 9.9% in 1899 to 3.9% of the whole population in York. About 40% of the working class population in York in 1936 were living below the minimum standard (inadequate income + non-essential expenditure). This was nearly 1/4 of the whole population. A tabulation of a comparison of the numbers living in primary poverty between 1899 and 1936 shows:

Table 7.2
People living in primary poverty, 1899 - 1936

1936			1899		
No.	% whole pop.	% low residents	No.	% whole pop.	% low residents
3767	3.9	6.8	7230	9.9	15.46

In 1950, Rowntree and Laver divided the families into the following classes according to their available income after paying rent and rates for a family of man, woman and three children:

Class

A <77s (equivalent to 33/6 in 1936)
B 77s & <100s
C 100s & <123s
D 123s & <146s
E 146s & over

As £5-0-2 was the primary poverty line for this type of family, then all those in classes A & B were the numbers living in poverty, as Table 7.3 shows:

Table 7.3
People living in primary poverty in 1950

Class	no. of PERSONS	% of working class pop.	% of total pop
A	234	0.37	0.23
B	1512	2.40	1.43
-------------POVERTY	---------------	---------------LINE	---------------
C	12096	19.23	11.48
D	36585	58.24	34.98

Class	no. of FAMILIES	% of working class pop.	% of total pop.
A	81	0.41	
B	765	4.23	
-------------POVERTY	---------------	---------------LINE	---------------
C	3510	19.40	
D	3141	17.38	
E	10602	58.58	(pp. 29/34)

So in 1950, 2.77% of the working class population and 1.66% of the total population of York, measured in individuals, were living in primary poverty. The family measurement was correspondingly, 4.64% of the working class population. There were 846 families in York living in primary poverty. Rowntree and Laver made the interesting observation that not a single family was in poverty due to the unemployment of the able-bodied wage earner. (p. 34) They went on to delve into this significant finding by explaining that the reduction of unemployment to negligible proportions had been a factor of considerable importance in the reduction of poverty from its comparatively high level in 1936 to the low level we found in 1950. They sought to examine how far a substantial amount of unemployment would have affected the situation disclosed by their investigations. Accordingly, they took all their schedules relating to families where the head of household was in employment and placed them in a pile of no particular order. They then drew every 20th schedule out of the pile. On each of the schedules thus selected, they disregarded the information about the earnings of the head of household and substituted a sum representing the unemployment benefit he would have received under the National Insurance Act if he were unemployed. They were thus able to calculate what proportion of the working class families in York would have been in each of their classes A to E if 5% of the heads of households were unemployed. The results were as follows:

Class	Actual situation in 1950 % (families)	Situation with 5% unemployed % (families)
A	0.41	1.89
B	4.23	5.72
C	19.40	19.74
D	17.38	16.96
E	58.58	55.69
		(pp. 46/7)

Then they made similar calculations, but drawing out of the pile every tenth schedule, thus showing what the situation would have been if 10% of the heads of households were unemployed. That would have represented 'a fairly serious degree of unemployment' and the results of their calculations can be seen below:

Class	Actual situation in 1950 % (families)	Situation with 10% unemployed % (families)
A	0.41	3.43
B	4.23	7.12
C	19.40	20.05
D	17.38	16.50
E	58.58	52.90
		(p. 47)

Finally to obtain the best possible comparison with 1936, they made random selections from their schedules on such a scale as to represent a situation which would have arisen if 8.8% of the heads of households were unemployed. They chose this figure because it was the actual level of unemployment in York in 1936. The results were as follows:

Class	Actual situation in 1950	Situation if unemployment had been at same level in 1936
	% (families)	%Families
A	0.41	2.64
B	4.23	6.47
C	19.40	19.94
D	17.38	16.80
E	58.58	54.15

Thus if unemployment in York in 1950 had been at the same level as in 1936, 9.11% of working class families would have been in poverty. In these families, there were 4,934 individuals, equivalent to 7.85% of the working class population. Although this study does not, because it cannot, measure the proportions of 'the working class' in poverty, these estimates are of important relevance, given the extent of unemployment in Britain today. When our conclusions are considered, it may be that a predictable response might point to the high unemployment levels brought on by the recession as the main causal factor of the enormous increase in the numbers of people in primary poverty. But when that variable is controlled, as Rowntree and Laver's estimates help us do, it is worth bearing their figures in mind to compare with our findings in order to quantify the contribution made by mass unemployment to the extent of poverty - and indeed to conclude that the extent of unemployment in 1992 can only partially explain the substantial increase. In 1936-9, 31.1% of the working class population **ONLY** were in poverty, whilst in 1950, 7.85% of the working class population **ONLY** were living in poverty. (pp. 48/9) They saw no reason why the three previous tables should not represent accurately the situation in their three hypothetical cases, but they pointed out that if unemployment were at all prolonged, various factors would operate which would tend to upset their calculations. The principal of these factors were:

(1) Where payments became due on H.P. of furniture or to building societies.

(2) Many families, renting dwellings, particularly those in the more expensive council houses, would no doubt have given them up in a time of prolonged unemployment and would have lived more cheaply with relatives and friends.

(3) School meals, for which, in all except the poorest families, children were made to pay at a rate of 2/6 per week, would no doubt have been given free to those whose fathers were in poverty through unemployment.

(4) Substantial unemployment of the heads of households would probably have reduced the number of women who had taken jobs to supplement their husband's earnings.

(5) Their poverty line income included allowances for clothing and for household sundries. Except in long periods of unemployment, many of these purchases could have been postponed without any serious effects, in order to allow the available income to be concentrated on the most essential items of expenditure.

(pp. 48/9)

Thus to measuring the extent of primary poverty in Britain in 1992 using the primary poverty line established by this research exercise. Data obtained from the Households Below Average Income (Dept. of Social Security) tables help us to uncover the extent of primary poverty experienced by families with children. The money values of weekly incomes of quintile medians for couples with children (after housing costs) are shown in table 7.4.

Table 7.4
Weekly income quintile medians of couples with children

1992 prices	Bottom	Second	Third	Whole
£ per week	78	129	168	193

In an attempt to equate our poverty line with the relevant income group and family type, it was necessary to investigate the breakdown of families within this group:

Table 7.5
Analysis of family type within income quintile groups

	Bottom Quintile	Second Quintile	Third Quintile	Whole
Couple + 1 child	22	25	30	31
Couple + 2 children	**36**	**46**	**49**	**44**
Couple + 3 children	22	18	18	17
Couple + 4 or more children	20	11	3	8

Table 7.5 shows that 42% of bottom quintile had three or more children, whilst only 22% had one child, with the biggest group by far being our 'moderate family' with two children. In the second quintile, 29% of families with children had three or more, 25% had one child, with families with two children again being, by far, the most common type at 46%. We can therefore validly apply our primary poverty line for a man, woman and two children to all families with children on the grounds that:

- this family is substantially more common than any other type and;
- there are significantly more families with three or more children than with only one child and thus, we are, in all likelihood, **under-estimating** the extent of primary poverty among British families with dependent children.

(As the study progresses, it is the aim of the research to estimate a primary poverty line for **all types** of families, from a young single householder, to a couple without children, to a single parent with children, to a couple with up to six or seven children, to a single pensioner and retired couple. As single pensioners, single parent families and couples with more than one child constitute, by far, the largest proportions of households in poverty, the findings of this pilot study will certainly prove to be an **under-estimation**.

But clearly from these tables, at this stage, we can safely say that **at least 30% (half way between the median income groups of the bottom and second quintiles) of families with two children are living on or below a 1992 primary poverty line, constructed upon the approaches and ethos or B.S. Rowntree.** We can also say that this measurement can be applied to all families with children - but this is likely to be an under-estimation; and social trends suggest that, when a primary poverty yardstick is put together for all household types, the likelihood is that the rate of 30% will not be reduced and indeed, may very well increase.

Our primary poverty line of £129.78 compares very unfavourably with the average weekly expenditure among similarly constituted families at £320.50; or among all such families with a normal weekly household income of under £275 of £231.25. The corresponding figures with deductions for alcohol and tobacco are £303.78 (all similar family types) and £214.05 (incomes below £275). (Family Spending 1992) Other research has recently been published by the Family Budget Unit at York which constructed a budget standard described as 'low cost' / breadline and which had been pared to a bare minimum and implied 'a very boring lifestyle'. Their findings suggested that the same 'moderate family' consisting of a couple with two children require £141 per week (or £350 a week for a 'modest but adequate' standard of living). That would allow for a fridge but no microwave oven, a TV but no music system, a child's bike but no car, cinema but no pantomine, and a day trip to the seaside but not an annual holiday. The fact that this standard is almost £12 a week higher than the primary poverty line put together here reinforces the bare minimum nature of our estimates.

Comparison of Rowntree's measurements of primary poverty in York throughout the first half of the 20th century with primary poverty as measured by a standard costed in Liverpool in 1992 may appear rather contrived and inaccurate. However, we again look to Rowntree for support and validity. His initial study in 1899 was, first and foremost, an attempt to test whether the abject poverty which Charles Booth found in London in the 1880s was comparable in its extent to provincial cities such as Rowntree's own York. In a letter written to Rowntree on July 25th 1901, Booth commented: 'I certainly think that the slight difference in our methods ought in no way to prevent the possibility of a comparison being made between your results and mine ... our totals may be correctly compared and the comparison you have shown is very close. At this I am not surprised. I have indeed long thought that other cities, if similarly tested, would show a percentage of poverty not differing greatly from that existing in London.' (Rowntree BS. 1903, p.5) And R. Nash, in reviewing Rowntree's book for the Women's Co-operative Guild in 1902 (p. 3) stated: 'There is no reason to suppose that things are worse in York than elsewhere. On the contrary, York is a city where there is plenty of employment ... it is clearly in a more favourable position than some other places.' Booth and Rowntree (and Nash) thus perceived no great invalidity in comparing poverty in London and York, as they employed broadly similar research techniques and approaches. Correspondingly, as Liverpool / Merseyside is probably **the** most deprived area in Britain and as we applied our estimates costed in Liverpool to national data, again this points to a likely under-estimation in our comparisons.

The next table shows the increase in primary poverty throughout the 20th century, from Rowntree's studies in 1899, 1936/41 and 1950 to the present primary poverty in Britain in 1992, as determined by this study. It must again be pointed out that the Rowntree figures for 1899, 1936/41 and 1950 in Table 7.6 relate to the whole population of York, while the 1992 'Rowntree Re-visited' level refers to families with two dependent children, nation-wide. We have attempted to rationalise and justify this in pages 113/4:

Table 7.6
Primary poverty in the twentieth century

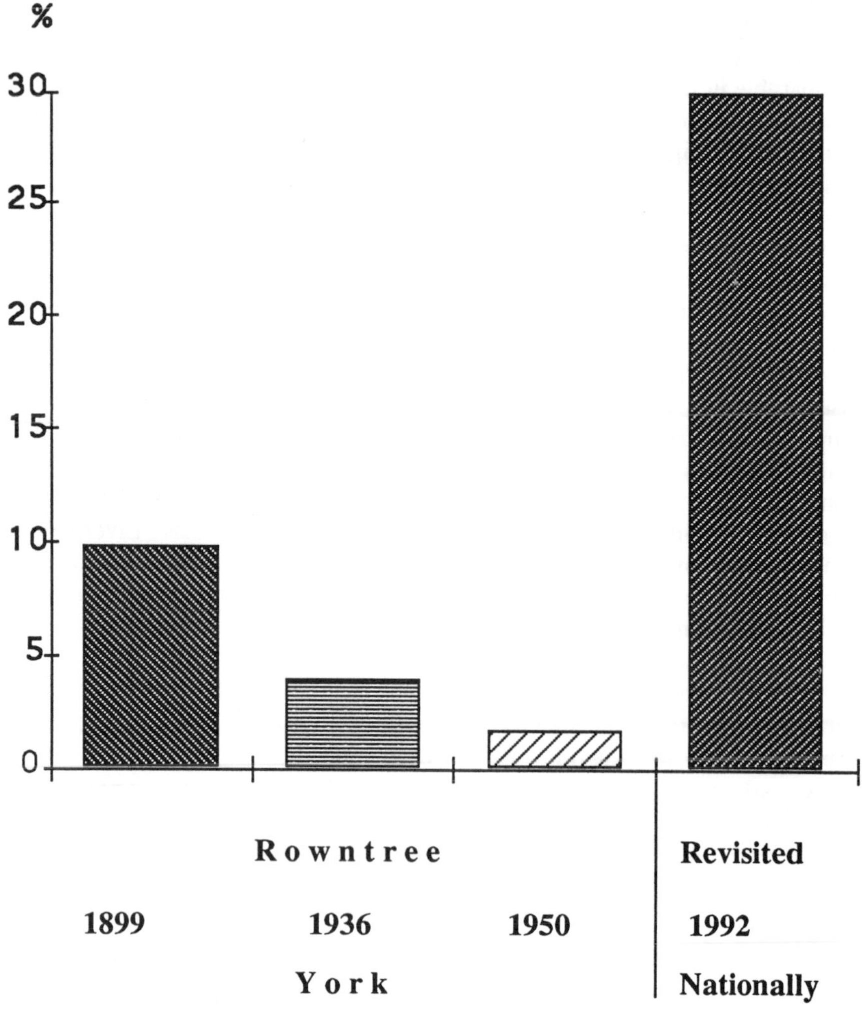

8 Concluding remarks

Rowntree emphatically drove home his underlying approach time and time again: 'It cannot ... be too clearly understood nor too emphatically repeated that **whenever a worker having three children dependent upon him and receiving not more than 21s./8d. per week indulges in any expenditure beyond that required for the barest physical needs, he can do so only at the cost of his own physical efficiency, or that of some members of his family**'. (pp. 134/5) This research asserts that whenever a family with two children with a weekly income of £129.78 spends money on items not required for subsistence in 1992, this will inevitably result in some damage to their physical efficiency.

Again in pre-empting potentially critical remarks from the middle-class audience to whom he was addressing his research:

> Some readers may be inclined to say, upon reading the above, 'This surely is an over-statement. Look at the thousands of families with incomes of 18s. to 21s., or even less, where the men do smoke and do spend money upon drink and the women do spend money on dress and recreation, and yet, in spite of it all, they seem happy and contented and the men make good workmen!'. Such arguments against the actual pressure and consequences of poverty will however, upon closer investigation, be found to be illusory. They come among a class of arguments against which

> Bastiat, the French economist, warned his readers in a series of articles entitled "That Which is Seen & That Which is Not Seen". In these articles, the writer pointed out the danger of forming judgements upon social and economic questions without thoroughly investigating them. In the argument referred to above, the money spent by the poor on drink, dress or recreation is one of the 'things that are seen'. There are however, consequences of poverty which are 'not seen'. We see that many a labourer who has a wife and three or four children, is healthy and a good worker, although he only earns £1 a week. What we do not see is that in order to give him enough food, mother and children habitually go short, for the mother knows that all depends upon the wages of her husband. We see the man go to the public house and spend money on drink; we do not see the children going supperless to bed in consequence. These unseen consequences of poverty have however to be reckoned with - the high death rate among the poor, the terribly high infant mortality, the stunted stature and dulled intelligence - all these and others are not seen unless we look beneath the surface; and yet all are having their effect upon the poor and consequently upon the whole country. (pp. 135/6)

We ask the reader to apply these sentiments and beliefs to our own research message, particularly as this exercise has specifically excluded the costs of drinking and smoking from the estimates and has allowed only a bare minimum for recreation and for clothing.

Turning to the general moral and economic questions which he felt his research generated:

> As the investigations into the life in this typical provincial town has proceeded, the writer has become increasingly impressed with the gravity of the facts which have unfolded themselves. That in this land of abounding wealth, during a time of perhaps unexampled prosperity, probably more than one quarter of the population are living in poverty is a fact which may well cause great searching of heart. There is surely need for a greater concentration of thought by the nation upon the well-being of its own people, for no civilisation can be sound or stable which has, at its base, this mass of stunted human life. The suffering may well be all but voiceless and we may long remain ignorant of its extent and severity, but when once we realise it, we see that social questions of profound importance await solutions. What, for instance, are the prime causes of this poverty? How far is it the result of false social and economic conditions? If it be due to faults in part of the national character, what influences can be exerted to impart to that character, greater strength and thoughtfulness? The object of the writer however has been to state the facts

rather than suggest remedies. He desires nevertheless to express his belief that however difficult the path of social progress may be, a way of advance will open out before patient and penetrating thought, if inspired by a true human sympathy. The dark shadow of Malthusian philosophy has passed away and no view of the ultimate scheme of things would now be accepted under which men and women are doomed by inevitable law to a struggle for existence so severe as necessarily to cripple or destroy the higher parts of their nature.' (pp. 304/5)

The conclusion of this piece of work suggests that 'the dark shadow of Malthusian philosophy' has certainly not passed away - or at least, has returned to haunt the socio-economic structure of modern Britain as we approach the 21st century. Commenting on Rowntree's 1899 work, R. Nash of the Women's Co-operative Guild (1902, p.3) stated: 'Mr. Rowntree's book ... is a very important one, affecting as it does people's whole attitude on questions of citizenship and on the right relation of the prosperous self-helping workers to the wretched inhabitants of the slums.' Again in asking the reader to apply Rowntree's above statement to the conditions of the poorest in Britain in the 1990s, the conditions of Britain's poor in the 1990s can be contextualised within the 'in vogue' academic and political concept of social citizenship, the classic definition of which was offered by T.H. Marshall in (1952): 'By the social element I mean the whole range, from a right to a modicum of economic welfare and security to the right to share to the full in the social heritage and to live the life of a civilised being, according to the standard prevailing in society.'

The emphasis on needs as well as rights acknowledges that everyone has basic needs and a requirement for, at the very least, 'a modicum of economic welfare and security' which, if not fulfilled will disentitle them from their most basic rights. These rights present at two fundamental levels: (a) to participate fully in social life with self-respect and with the respect of others; (b) the satisfaction of basic needs such as an adequate diet, proper clothing, a warm home etc. It has been this latter definition upon which this research has concentrated and the exercise has exposed the extent of the denial of even the most fundamental citizenship rights to the poorest. Poor people lack the resources to fulfil what is expected of them as national citizens, in the workplace, in the community, and thus, they are also denied the opportunities to fulfil the obligations and duties as equal citizens.

If an important element of social citizenship is the 'opportunities to make choices', (Dahrendorf R. 1976) these choices for the poor are absent when it comes to deciding what is for dinner, whether to turn the heating on or not, to 'eat or heat', whether or not to buy a new pair of shoes for the children etc.

If freedom of choice is an important element of citizenship, then this research has demonstrated that primary poverty has curtailed such freedom in a most swingeing way. The freedom to eat healthily as and one wishes, to go where and when one likes, to pursue the leisure activities which are necessary for a modest degree of variability, all are denied to those who cannot afford them. According to Tyneside CPAG:

> The picture which emerges from this detailed study of family life is one of constant restriction in almost every aspect of people's activities ... The lives of these families, and perhaps most seriously, the lives of the children in them, are marked by the unrelieved struggle to manage, with dreary diets and drab clothing. They also suffer what amounts to cultural imprisonment in their home in our society in which getting out with money to spend on recreation and leisure is normal at every other income level ... Clearly (their income) is not enough to allow ordinary families to share in conventional living standards.

The scientific results of this research reinforce and deepen this picture and argue that poverty is even more primary than such an anecdotal image offered by most poverty studies. It is concluded that, for millions of families with children, poverty means the exclusion from the standards of living and the lifestyles, not just of one's fellow citizens, but also of that deemed as the lowest upon which citizens in a civilised society should be expected to subsist. 'Properly understood, a poor citizen is a contradiction in terms.' (Vincent D. 1991, p. 205)

We acknowledge that many criticisms will be levelled against our inclusion or exclusion of many items, their quantities and their costs. However, we reply with Rowntree's (1903, p. 27) cover that: 'To say that our statements are not beyond microscopic criticism, that they do not fully cover the ground, is not sufficient to discredit them. Criticism is valuable in the measure of its strict accuracy and scrupulous justice.'

As this project has suggested, poverty research need not involve the most up-to-date highly complex methodologies and technicalities. Indeed operating such approaches often serves to sanitise and distance a very tragic and emotive human experience. This piece of poverty bears a simplistic imagination in that it is purely a replication of the famous research exercise by Rowntree. Previous research need not be forsaken merely on the grounds that it is old hat; rather lessons should be learned from it. The voluminous and exhaustive research carried out by Townsend (1979) and Mack & Lansley (1985 & 1991) did not provoke a batting of the eye-lid by the policy-making process; whereas Rowntree's research is credited with encouraging and influencing the Liberal

Reforms of 1906/11 and with persuading Beveridge to use a needs-based approach to establishing the social security scale rates in the 1940s. If this research provokes a tiny fraction of the changes in policy and attitudes which followed Rowntree's research, then it will have been worthwhile.

Bibliography

Barker P. (1984): *'Founders of the Welfare State'*, Heinemann.

Berthoud R. & Kempson E. (1992): *'Credit and Debt:* the PSI Report', Policy Studies Institute, London.

Boardman B. (1991): *'Fuel Poverty: From Cold Homes to Affordable Warmth'*, Belhaven press.

Bowley A.L. & Hogg M.H. (1925): *'Has Poverty Diminished?'*, King, London.

BRESCU Henderson. (1991): *'Energy Efficiency Means Warmer Homes at No Extra Cost'*, Information leaflet 11 Sept. 1989 (updated 1991).

Briggs A. (1961): *'Social Thought & Social Action: A Study of the Work of Seebohm Rowntree'*, Longman, London.

Church of England (1985): *'Faith in the City'*, Church House.

Cohen R. (1991): *'Just About Surviving: Debt and the Social Fund'*, Family Service Units, Bradford.

Cohen R., Coxall J., Craig G. & Sadiq-Sangster A. (1992): *'Hardship Britain'*, CPAG.

Cole-Hamilton I. & Lang T. (1986): *'Tightening Belts: A report on the Impact of Food Poverty in London'*, London Food Commission.

Cole-Hamilton I. (1991): *'Poverty Can Seriously Damage Your Health'*, CPAG.

Collins KJ. (1986): *'The Health of the Elderly in Low Income Temperatures'*, Institute of Environmental Health Officers and Legal Research Institute, Warwick, Dec. 14-16.

COMA (1984): *'Diet and Cardiovascular Disease'*, (A report on health and social subjects No. 28), DHSS.

COMA (1991): *'Dietery Reference Values for Food Energy and Nutrients for the United Kingdom'*, (A report on health and social subjects No. 41), DHSS.

Crawley H. (1988): *'Food Portion Sizes'* HMSO.

Central Statistical Office (1992): *'Family Spending'* A report on the 1991 family expenditure survey', HMSO.

Central Statistics Office (1992): *'Social Trends 22'*, HMSO.

Dahrendorf R. (1976): *'Inequalities, Hope & Progress'*, Univ. of Liverpool Press.

Davey-Smith G., Bartley M. & Blane D. (1990): *'The Black Report on Socio-economic Inequalities in Health, 10 years On'*, British Medical Journal Vol. 301, 18-25 Aug.

Department of the Environment, Energy Efficiency Office (1992): *'Insulating Your Home'*, Autumn.

Department of the Environment, Energy Efficiency Office (1992): *'Heating Your Home'*, Autumn.

Department of the Environment (1991): *'Attitudes to Energy Conservation in the Home'*, HMSO.

Department of Health (1989): *'Dietary Sugars and Human Diseases'*, (Report

Department of Health (1989): *'Dietary Sugars and Human Diseases'*, (Report on health and social subjects No. 37) HMSO.

Department of Social Security (1990): *'Households Below Average Income 1988/89: a statistical analysis'*, HMSO.

EEO (1986): *'Cutting Home Energy Cost: A step by step monergy guide'*, (Gas), (Electricity), Energy Efficiency Office, London.

Family Budget Unit (1992): *'Household Budgets and Living Standards'*, Joseph Rowntree Foundation, November, York.

Field F. (1982): *'Poverty & Politics'* Heinemann, London.

Fox BA. & Cameron AG. (Date): *'Food Science, Nutrition and Health'*, 5th edition, Edward Arnold.

Hanes FA. & De Looy AE. (1987): *'Can I Afford the Diet?'*, Human Nutrition: Applied Nutrition, 41A, 1-12.

Hennock EP. (1987): *'The Measurement of Poverty: From the Metropolis to the Nation, 1880-1920'*, The Economic History Review, Second Series, Vol. XL, May.

Johnson P. & Webb S. (1990): *'Poverty in Official Statistics: Two Reports'*, Joseph Rowntree Foundation, October.

Leather S. (1992): *'By Bread Alone'*, Ministry of Agriculture, Fisheries and Foods, Working paper CP (92) 9/8.

Leather S. (1992): *'The Politics of the Right and Wrong Food'*, Unpublished monograph for National Consumer Council, October.

Liverpool City Council (1991): *'The Liverpool Quality of Life Survey'*, June.

Marshall T.H. (1952): *'Citizenship & Social Class'*, CUP.

McCabe M. (1992), *'Establishing a Clothing Budget for Three Family Types'*, Family Budget Unit, York.

Ministry of Agriculture, Food & Fisheries (1989): *'Manual of Nutrition'*, 4th edition, HMSO.

Ministry of Agriculture, Food & Fisheries (1990): *'Household Food Consumption & Expenditure 1990: Annual Report of the National Food Survey Committee'*, HMSO.

Ministry of Agriculture, Food & Fisheries (1992): *'The Cost of Alternative Diets'*, Ministry of Agriculture, Fisheries and Foods, Food science division, Working paper CP (92) 9/3

Mintel (1987): *'Market Intelligence'*, March.

Mintel (1992): *'Market Intelligence'*, February.

Nash R. (1902): *'How the Poor Live'*, Women's Co-operative Guild.

National Association of Citizen Advice Bureaux (1992): *'CAB Evidence: The Cost of Living'*, NACAB, December.

National Consumer Council (1992): *'Your Food: Whose Choice?'*, HMSO

National Children's Home (1992): *'Deep in Debt: A Survey of Problems Faced by Low Income Families'*, October.

National Advisory Council on Nutritional Education (NACNE) (1983): *'A Discussion Paper on Proposals for Nutritional Guidelines for Health Education in Britain'*, Health Education Council.

Oppenheim C. (1993): *'Poverty: The Facts'*, CPAG.

O'Shaughnessy A. (1992): *'Report on Schoolchildren, Food and Health Seminar'*, Liverpool Healthy City 2000 Project.

Rowntree B.S. (1901): *'Poverty: A Study of Town Life'*, MacMillan

Rowntree B.S. (1903): *'The Poverty Line: A Reply'*, Henry Good.

Rowntree B.S. (1937): *'The Human Needs of Labour'*, Longman.

Rowntree B.S. (1941): *'Poverty & Progress'*, Longman.

Rowntree B.S. & Laver G.R. (1951): *'Poverty & the Welfare State'* Longman.

Stitt S. (1989): *'Supplementary Benefits: A Test of Adequacy by Disaggregation'*, PhD. Thesis, Queens University, Belfast.

Stitt S. (1991): *'Of Little Benefit'*, Campaign against Poverty.

Stitt S. (1992): *'B.S. Rowntree & Supplementary Benefits: A Comparative Analysis'*, Liverpool Polytechnic.

Townsend P. (1979): *'Poverty in the U.K.'*, Penguin.

Tyneside CPAG (1990): *'Living on the Edge'*, CPAG.

Van-Beuren G., (1992): CPAG Annual Conference, November, York.

Veit Wilson J. (1986): *'Paradigms of Poverty - A Rehabilitation of B.S. Rowntree'*, Journal of Social Policy, vol. 15, part 1.

Veit Wilson J. (1987): *'Consensual Approaches to Poverty Lines & Social Security'*, Journal of Social Policy, vol. 16, part 2.

Vincent D. (1991): *'Poor Citizens'*, Longman.

Ward, Wackman, Wartella (1977): *'How Children Learn'*, Sage.

Williams DRR. (1987): *'Why Wait Any Longer for a National Food Policy?'*, Journal of the Royal Society of Medicine, Vol. 80, April.

Wenlock RW., Buss DH. & Derry BJ. (1986): *'Household Food Wastage in Britain'*, British Journal of Nutrition 43.